F. Barton Davis

Closer Than a Brother

Unlocking the Secrets of the One Another Way

www.magimediapub.com

Close Than a Brother

Copyright © 2008 by F. Barton Davis

Published by Magi Media Publications

P. O. Box 332

Pelham Al 35124

Printed in the United States

Cover design: CGKmdia

Interior design: CGKmedia

ISBN 978-0-9819502-0-4

To my lovely wife Michelle, my best friend and personal hero. You make me better and call me higher. And to my Mom for always believing in me and inspiring me.

Contents

FOREWARD

Have you ever read something that both encouraged you and provoked you at the same time? That was my response to Frank's book. I was encouraged by his clarity and insight as he addressed a sensitive and timely subject. I was provoked by his forthrightness in challenging us to move forward as we learn from our past mistakes. Positive provocation is needed at times to move us to action (Hebrews 10:24).

The purpose of this book is **not** to dwell on the past but to reasonably and thoughtfully examine our relationships with one another. Closer Than a Brother points us to the future. The encouragement in the book to "extend grace" is essential as we rebuild not only our relationships but also our churches. Frank's use of scripture and reason spurs us to examine our past and present relationships through the prism of God's love and forgiveness.

Frank and I have known each other for many years. I am thankful Frank has been gracious with me as well as open and honest. My wife and I were in a discipling relationship with

Frank and his wife for several years and we love him and Michelle very much. I greatly admire his unrelenting pursuit of the truth. Honestly, this quality could be exasperating at times (if you know Frank you know what I mean) but in the end, much appreciated. As I was reading Frank's book, I would sometimes be reminded of Rodney Dangerfield's retort, "I resemble that remark." In fact, I think most of us will relate to his descriptive views and personal accounts.

This book can also be used as a practical tool for teaching and group work. "Unlocking the secrets of the one another way" is vital to our personal spiritual health and to the growth of the Lord's church. Frank has certainly given us some important keys to unlocking these truths.

Donald A. Burroughs, M.A., LAPC
Evangelist/Counselor
Savannah Church of Christ

Introduction

I grew up in a fairly religious family and spent my childhood attending church and not just one denomination; I experienced a cross section of contemporary Christianity. My Mom grew up in a little A.M.E. church, in the country, so a few of our family reunions and holidays were spent there. She converted to Catholicism before I was born, so we frequently attended Catholic parishes. I even completed several of the sacraments, but we were pretty uncommitted Catholics, so we visited all different kinds of fellowships, Baptist, Episcopal, Lutheran, etc. When I entered high school, one of my brothers and I started playing in a Christian band. We played in churches all over Baltimore (my hometown), and whatever denominations I hadn't visited up to that point, we played for; Pentecostal, Holiness, small predominantly white churches, even big African-American mega-churches.

It's funny, I grew up liking church, but the more I matured, the more different groups I visited, the more I began to resent and distrust organized religion.   I saw little difference between my teen friends who went to church and claimed to be Christians and the ones who didn't. We all did the same things and got involved in the same mess Monday through Saturday, with the only real difference being what we did for a few hours on Sunday morning. I saw even more disturbing hypocrisy among the adults, choir directors sleeping around, preachers skimming money, friends catching the Spirit on Sunday morning and cursing each other out Sunday night. What was the point? How was this being born again? By the time I went to college, I had made the decision to stop attending church altogether except for when I came home on holidays (My mom was an old school mom, so going to church on Sunday was not optional). I was seriously disillusioned with organized religion. There were too many denominations, too much holy talk, and too little holy living.

Unfortunately, I don't think my story is unique. The truth is, modern Christianity is adrift. Countless denominations teach variations of the plan of salvation, different standards of commitment, and even wildly different moral standards. In numerous congregations, complacency and indifference have become the norm rather than the exception. Eight years into a new millennium, Sunday morning is still the most racially segregated hour of the week. Races that work together, go to school together, and die on the battlefield together still largely worship the Son of God separately.   There seems to be an enormous disconnect between the Christianity of the scriptures and what comprises our reality. The question facing us is simple: Is the Bible our standard or our ideal?

Acts 2:42-47 describes the early days of the first century church.   It reads: *"They devoted themselves to the apostles teachings and to fellowship to the breaking of bread and to prayer. Everyone was filled with awe, and many wonders and miraculous signs were done by the apostles. All the believers were together and had everything in common. Selling their possessions and goods, they gave to anyone as he had need. Every day they continued to meet together in the temple courts. They broke bread together with glad and sincere hearts, praising God and enjoying the favor of all the people. And the Lord added to their numbers daily those who were being saved."*

This passage describes a church defined by its devotion to Christ and to each other. It was a congregation that functioned as family, meeting each other's needs and having intimate friendships that extended far outside of assembly for worship. Their closeness is even more amazing when one understands that a few verses earlier, the scriptures inform us that the members of this fellowship were from all over the known world.

Miracles followed these disciples and in spite of persecution, they experienced growth that was both incredible and consistent. What an amazing testimony to the greatness of God!

If this passage is meant to be an ideal, it puts no pressure on us, but if it is a blueprint for how Christ 's church should be, everywhere and for every generation, it functions as both an inspiration and an indictment. I believe that Acts 2:42-47 is a blueprint for the Lord's church. It is what we are called to be, what we must become. That conviction both challenges me and gives me hope that attaining that standard of love, commitment, and devotion in the church today is possible. What stops this from being our reality? What is the missing ingredient? A large part of the problem is that we have yet to truly tap into the power of the one another way.

What is the one another way and what is its relevance to the Christian walk and the health of God's church? What is its relationship to discipling? Are they one and the same? Is discipling a fabricated word representing a man made structure or does it have its roots in scripture? Answering these questions is of the utmost importance because the one another way represents the brick and mortar that holds Christ's church together. It is a fundamental building block for restoring the Christianity of the Bible.

The one another way is the narrow road, the glory road, purchased by the cross and powered by the resurrection. It is the key to unlocking the power of Christ's love in our lives and in His modern day church. The goal of this book is to bring the one another passages to life so that all of us can apply them to our lives and let them transform us, transform God's church and like our predecessors in the first century, to once more, turn the whole world upside down. There are few subjects more important. It is time to cut through the uncertainty, grab hold of the scriptures and unveil the secrets of the one another way.

The Narrow Door

What is the one another way? What is discipling? Is it Biblical? Should it be structured? How can it be implemented without becoming hierarchical? Was it practiced during Biblical times? If so, how? Before we can answer any of these questions we have a far more pressing one. What is a Christian and how does someone become one?

This may seem unnecessary. Surely, we all know what it means to be a Christian, right? I've been saved for twenty-four years and have been a preacher for twenty-two, and in that time have talked with countless people about their walk with God. It is amazing how many radically different answers I hear to those two basic questions. What is a Christian? How is someone saved?

For the past few years, my family and I lived in Atlanta, Ga., and I discovered that Atlanta is an extremely religious city.

Everyone you meet is a member of someone's church and that's how they tend to word it, "I belong to Bishop So and So's church, or to the apostle Sugar Daddy's church, etc." I've spent quite a few years living in both New York and Atlanta. Do you want to know the difference between the two? In New York everyone you meet claims to be in the entertainment industry. Your waitress claims that she's really a dancer; your cabdriver claims that he is really an actor; even your dentist claims that he's really a rapper, going by the alias M.C. Grillz. If you have ever lived in the big apple, you know that this is true. In Atlanta it is different. Here, everyone claims to be a realtor and a preacher. Your plumber, your hairdresser, and even your local podiatrist all sell real estate on the side and claim to preach occasionally at somebody's church. It is the only city that I know of where every individual at a crime scene claims to be saved and be a member of the same mega-church. The police officer, the shop clerk, and even the thief, are all members in good standing. With all these "saved people", all these churchgoing folk, shouldn't that be reflected in the lifestyle and behavior of the city? Everybody claims to be a member of a church so why is there bumper to bumper traffic on Monday thru Friday, but no traffic on the road Sunday morning? The answer is pretty simple. Holy talk does not necessarily equate to holy living. There is a massive disconnect between how many individuals define Christianity and how Jesus does.

When I enrolled in college, I didn't know much scripture, even though I'd gone to church my entire life. I knew the standard fare, John 3:16 and Romans 10:9-10 and not much else. I knew enough to know that something was wrong. What I had seen at church simply did not seem to relate to what little I knew about Jesus. Why would Jesus endure so much for us to be the same people we had always been? Shouldn't there be a distinction between Christ's church and the world? My solution was to quit going to church and just worship God my own way (that normally included praying to Saint Mattress on Sunday mornings). Eventually, a guy on campus who kept inviting me to a Bible discussion group, wore me down after inviting me a million times over the course of a semester. I finally attended and what I heard changed my life. I learned about the narrow door (Matthew 7:13:14, Luke 13:22-25).

Matthew 7:13-14 states, " *Enter through the narrow gate. For broad is the road that leads to destruction, and many enter through it. But small is the gate and narrow the road that leads to life, and only a few find it*".

The reality of modern day Christianity is that it has chosen the broad road. It has chosen salvation without sacrifice, the cross without commitment, and rebirth without first dying to self. Over two thousand years of watering down the message, has left us with a gospel that is severely diluted, gospel-light, the fast food version for a fast food culture. Before we can talk about the one another way, we must understand and embrace true Christianity, and true Christianity begins with understanding what it means to be a disciple of Jesus.

In an age where the term Christian is applied to people with even a nominal belief in Jesus, it is important that we define what it means to be a believer the way Jesus does in the scriptures. From a Biblical perspective, one cannot be saved without being a disciple of Jesus (John 8:31-32). How do we know this? The word disciple is used in the New Testament well over two hundred times, but the word Christian is used in the entire Bible only three times, and its first use (Acts 11:25-26), approximately eleven years after the birth of the church, uses the term Christian as a synonym for being Christ's disciple. A Biblical definition of a Christian is simply a baptized disciple of Jesus. In other words, one can believe, go to church, sing in the choir, and be no more saved than a devout atheist. Usually, discipleship is the missing ingredient. Discipleship is the byproduct of total surrender to Christ. It is a decision to follow in His steps wholeheartedly, at any cost. In Matthew 7:13-14, Jesus commands us to enter through the narrow door. Discipleship is what makes the narrow door narrow.

The faith, trust and obedience that it takes to have true one another relationships can only be achieved by people who are born again, filled with the Holy Spirit, and committed to the Master and His mission.

How is someone born again? Well, in one sense it's all about the cross. The cross makes salvation possible. The blood of Christ is available to all. The cross is the center of God's plan for our redemption, the embodiment of His love, and the perfect expression of God's grace. It is available to all; yet, all are not saved. God has done His part. The issue of who is lost and who is saved comes down to our response. We must respond to the cross and obey the steps God commands us to take so that we can participate in Christ's death, burial, and resurrection. Faith, repentance, and baptism are the fundamental steps involved in Biblical conversion, but the essence of saving faith is discipleship and the heart of being a disciple is making a decision that Jesus is Lord. While not the only step, lordship is surely the heart of the matter. Once Jesus is truly Lord, everything else will follow. Lordship is the key that brings everything else to life.

Lordship Is a Salvation Issue:

What is lordship? It is the cornerstone of our response to God. Our complete surrender is what God has always demanded from those who would follow Him. It is the first of the Ten Commandments *(**Exodus 20:3** "You shall have no other gods before me");* it is the greatest command *(**Luke 10:27** "...Love the Lord your God with all your heart and with all your soul and with all your strength and with all your mind");* it is the foundation of true worship *(**Romans 12:1-2** "...Offer your bodies as living sacrifices, holy and pleasing to God-this is your spiritual act of worship").* Without lordship, baptism is simply a bath, our faith becomes diluted, and true repentance becomes impossible. Salvation is made possible through the cross, and because we are saved by grace, no decision, no act of obedience or devotion, apart from Christ's sacrifice, would have meaning. On Calvary, God took the first step, creating an opportunity for all men to be saved, but we must take the biblical steps to respond to Jesus in order to personally receive the gift of salvation. Surrender is at the core of a biblical response. Simply put, before Christ can be your Savior, He must first be your Lord and Master.

Lordship means that we completely surrender to the will of Christ and accept His total sovereignty over every area of our lives. It demands us to be willing to go anywhere, change anything, commit everything, and do anything that Jesus commands. We set no conditions and no limitations on our obedience. Jesus is truly our master. God does not require perfection, but He does require 100% commitment. He wants all of our heart, all of our mind, all of our strength, and all of our soul as a condition for having a personal relationship (Luke 10:27). This is His terms of peace (Luke 14:33). Someone who accepts these terms is a true disciple of Christ and the act of living a surrendered life is called discipleship.

Please, understand the issue is commitment not perfection. If we could be sinless, we would not need a savior, and we would not need grace. It took my wife, Michelle about five minutes (probably less) to realize that the man she married wasn't perfect. She doesn't expect perfection from me, but she demands that I be committed to her and only her. If on our wedding day, during our vows, the preacher had asked "Are you willing to be faithful to her and only her?" and I had answered, ""I'll try," would she have accepted that? Of course not. What if I had answered, "Michelle's my number one but my girlfriends', Sue, Nancy and Karen are going to be two through four," do you think that would have been well received? (In all likelihood, I'd still be recovering from bodily injury) No, Michelle expects complete faithfulness. She wants to be my one unrivaled love. She expects me to be devoted to her and only her, never having to wonder whether I'm flirting with co-workers, who I'm with, whether or not I'm coming home, or whose bed I'm sharing.   She is not expecting perfection, but she is demanding 100% devotion and I expect the same.   100% commitment, it is what spouses should expect from each other, what coaches demand from their athletes, and what bosses often demand from their employees.   Why should God tolerate less?   Why is it acceptable to be more devoted, to our jobs, families, education, even our favorite sports teams, than to the Lord (Luke 14:25-27)?   God is not interested in our leftovers (Malachi 1:6-14).   He does not want to be one of the four major food groups of our lives.   He deserves more.   He demands more.   He is lord of all or nothing at all.

This is a salvation issue.   Anyone who wishes to follow Jesus has to be willing to deny himself daily and die for Him (Luke 9:23-26).   In this passage, Jesus is not describing a super Christian. He is establishing the requirement to simply be Joe Disciple. The unwillingness to completely surrender is why the rich young ruler went away sad, missing out on eternal life (Mark 10:20-27).   In Revelation 2:1-5 the church in Ephesus is commended for its sound doctrine, its hard work and its perseverance; yet, Christ had one thing against it.   The church had forgotten its first love.   In spite of all its positive accomplishments, Christ was going to cease to recognize the Ephesus church as His church (remove their lamp stand) unless they repented and once more put Him first in their lives.   God will not tolerate being second, and He will not accept a relationship on those terms. Lordship is a matter of life and death.

When I first heard this, studying the Bible with a friend over twenty-four years ago, it scared me to death. It seemed radical, foreign to the comfortable religion I had known, but something in me knew that it was right. Not only did I know it was right, I knew that it made more sense than anything I had ever heard. Jesus died for a reason, setting an example for me so that I would follow in His steps. There was no power in the empty religion I had lived before, but I knew there was power in this.

Lordship Is Divisive:

> *"Do not suppose that I have come to bring peace to the earth. I did not come to bring peace, but a sword. For I have come to turn a man against his father, a daughter against her mother, a daughter-in-law against a mother-in-law a man's enemies will be the members of his own household,"* **Matthew 10:34-36.**

Jesus has always divided a room, for He is both the most loved and the most hated personality in the history of the world. In our day and age, nothing epitomizes this aspect of Jesus' teaching more than the issue of discipleship.

Lordship is the difference between being a true disciple and simply being religious. Religion is all about setting limits, what kind of limits depends largely on how religious an individual is. A person may only have a little bit of religion. Their limit is they give God Easter, Christmas, and New Year's Eve, and nothing else. A person may be extremely religious (church three times a week, tithing, helping the poor, etc.), but their limit is that they will never forgive a certain family member for what he or she has done. Regardless of the extent of spiritual activity, once we set limits on what we will do for Jesus, we cease to be disciples and become merely religious people. Jesus did not die for this. On the cross Jesus gave everything, and now, he expects nothing less from us. Empty religion will not save anyone and following a spiritual routine will never change the world; yet, a handful of true disciples can and will turn this world upside down (Acts 17:6). Lordship makes all the difference.

Being a living sacrifice is the difference between being a churchgoer and being a disciple, it is the difference between having good intentions and seeing real change, and it is the difference between a church being dead (Revelation 2:1-7) and being alive (Revelation 2:8-11). It is the hardest concept for many of us to grasp (most of us have never been as committed to anything as Jesus calls us to be to Him), and it is the easiest thing to lose. Lukewarmness is the natural state of man. No one has to strive to be complacent, but true surrender, takes daily rededication and focus. Habitually, we slip back into the custom of bowing down before the altar of self. If we are serious about following Christ, it is time that we nail ourselves to the cross and live a new life in Jesus.

This was a hard teaching over 2,000 years ago, and it still is, but there is no way around it. If we are not living a crucified life then we are living a lie. If our churches are not preaching this message, powerfully and boldly, we are preaching a half-truth and have emptied the cross of its power. The absence of strong teaching on lordship is the reason I left the "traditional church" and joined the "discipling movement" twenty-four years ago. Likewise, during these times, discipleship will either be the issue that unites God's church or the one that divides it. There simply is no middle ground.

It Is All or Nothing At All:

God's standard is that Jesus is Lord of all or nothing at all. He requires 100%, not 50%, not 80%, not even 99%. He doesn't request more than what we have, but He demands all of us. He will shape us, mold us, and change us, once we have sacrificed ourselves on His altar, but he demands that we hold nothing back. Discipleship is not a list of do's and don'ts; it is the state of surrender.

In over 22 years as a minister, I can honestly say that this is a rare teaching, the rarest teaching. Too often, churches have participated in the widening of the narrow door and allowed this teaching to be ignored or severely diluted. To follow Jesus, we must be willing to go anywhere, sacrifice anything, and do anything that He commands. He must be first above school, work, wives, children, security, freedom, comfort, opinions, and even life itself. Christ is lord of all or nothing at all. This is a radical teaching; it always has been. This is an unpopular teaching; it always has been. This is a divisive teaching; it always has been (Luke 12:49-53 also Matthew 10:32-39). Unpopular though it may be, it remains the only way.

Lordship and Discipling:

Anyone who has ever made this commitment, who has set his heart on Jesus being Lord, knows two things: It is the most rewarding life that one could live and it is the most challenging. It is a lot like being married. I've been married nineteen years, my wife is incredible, I adore her, and love being married. I'm having a lot more fun being married than I had being single. That being said, being married is the greater challenge. For it to be a joy, it is a daily struggle. No matter how well it's going, a little neglect and it will completely unravel. Discipleship is the same way.

Lordship is what makes the narrow door narrow. It is the dividing line between being religious and being a disciple. It is the hardest thing to get. Every part of our natural selves fights against and resists embracing it. It is the first thing we let go of when we are struggling.

We cannot do it on our own. We cannot live it out on our own. We need the Word, we need God's Spirit, and we need the support of our brothers and sisters. This is where discipling comes in, where the one another way comes in. Anyone who has really given Jesus all of his heart, mind, soul, and strength, has realized that to live a surrendered life, he sometimes needs his brothers and sisters to hold him up. I know personally, I need people to encourage me, teach me, and sometimes to call me back when I've given in to compromise. There will be no self-made men in heaven. What is the truth about discipling? Each of us must be committed to carrying the cross daily. No one can carry the cross for us, but we must root for each other, refresh each other and from time to time even carry each other, becoming mat bearers (Mark 2:3-5) if we are going to finish the race and claim the prize.

Lafayette Summers wrote a song for Deeper Shade of Soul's "Alive at the Roxy" CD entitled "Yes Lord"(Deeper Shade of

Soul is a gospel choir based in Atlanta). Here is an excerpt from that song:

Verse:

My Lord told me that He

Needed somebody to be

Sold out for Him each and every day.

Said He needed someone to sacrifice,

Someone willing to lay down his life

He asked me would I live the crucified life

And live each day by faith

Chorus:

I told Him,

Yes Lord. Yes Lord. Yes Lord.

Yes Lord, I will do your will

Yes I'll make the sacrifice

Yes I'll live the crucified life.

Yes!

I have to constantly ask myself, how is it really going? Does the song, "Yes Lord" describe my commitment to Jesus or am I holding back? Are there areas of my life that I have not surrendered? What does my life style say about my priorities? What does my schedule say? Have I set limits? Are there scriptures I simply refuse to obey? Are there scriptures that I have watered down? What would Jesus say to me today? Would He say that I am whole hearted or would he say that there is something in my life that I am putting before my relationship with Him? There is no job, no hobby, no person, no sin, no habit, and no hurt that we can let hinder us. <u>Faith without lordship is hollow</u>. Baptism without lordship is simply a bath. Repentance without lordship is impossible. Sacrifice without lordship is detestable (Isaiah 1: 10-17). Unrivaled devotion is the decision that forms the foundation of our spiritual walk. What are you prepared to do? In the words of Morpheus from the movie *The Matrix*, " Is it going to be the red pill or the blue pill?" What's it going to be Mr. Anderson? It is time that we all answered the call.

Until we have made the personal decision to surrender, discipling does not make a lot of sense. When we are holding on to self, one another involvement, even involvement that is respectful and loving, often feels like intrusion. Once we have made Jesus Lord, it becomes quite clear that to successfully run the race, we need running partners. *"As iron sharpens iron, so one man sharpens another,"* **Proverbs 27:17.** This passage is the basis of healthy one another relationships. Discipling is about forming deep, spiritual friendships where we help each other walk the walk and talk the talk. It is biblical; it is powerful; it is necessary. Come, let us walk the narrow road together, and as we do, we will discover the power of the one another way.

Why We Fail

I was baptized into Christ in November of 1983, during my sophomore year of college, after studying the Bible with some friends of mine on campus off and on for a year. For anyone attempting to guess my age based on that information, all you need to know is that I started college at five, a regular boy genius. Actually, I'm forty-three and I was baptized one month shy of my nineteenth birthday. The campus ministry I was a part of back then was a campus ministry which considered itself part of the "Discipling Movement" and it was dedicated to living out the one another scriptures and the principles of discipling.

I would be lying if I didn't share that I owe everything to Christ and more than I can ever say to brothers and sisters who have loved me, given advice to me, counseled me, taught me, and rebuked me. I thank God for mentors who discipled me, Craig Cornish, John Brush, Sam Powell, Don Burroughs, and many more. Our attempts to practice the one another passages from then until this present day have molded and shaped every aspect of my character and helped me forge life long friendships.

I've been around the "Discipling Movement" long enough to see it go from loose and friendship based to extremely structured and suffocating, to cloudy and unsure and yet I am thankful for all of it, the bad and the good. Sitting down with an open Bible and a few good friends, I learned to date with absolute purity, learned to trust God through adversity, learned sound theology, learned to repent of racial prejudice, learned to take responsibility for my tongue, and countless other life-changing lessons. I've also been hurt, treated harshly, disrespected, and utterly and completely frustrated and helped others experience the same. Yet, I am thankful for the Discipling Movement with all its flaws for God has used the bad and the good to instruct, encourage and discipline me. Through our successes and failures, God is moving us forward, calling us higher.

In my opinion, not nearly enough churches have failed at discipling. This is because not nearly enough of them have ever sought to practice it. The truth is, either these congregations have failed to understand the importance of the one another scriptures or they have not known how to practically apply them. A Notable exception has been a fellowship of churches I mentioned earlier, labeled the "Discipling Movement", which have earnestly attempted to restore discipling in their congregations. The successes and failures of this movement and the lessons learned from them are the chief inspirations for this book. At its heart, the Bible is a practical book, God's manual for teaching us how to have a relationship with Him. As we wholeheartedly seek to put the scriptures into practice, the scriptures shed its light, pointing us to victory and allowing us to see the areas where we have strayed. If we are to succeed in having biblical one another / discipling relationships, we first need to let the Word show us clearly how and why we fail.

What are the reasons that past attempts to restore Biblical discipling have struggled? The primary reason is that we failed to pay close enough attention to the scriptural model. In the Discipling Movement, the term discipling became a catch phrase that encompassed mentoring relationships and the practical application of the New Testament one another passages. In the early days of the movement, members acquired prayer partners who helped spur each other on. As time progressed, a more structured system of mentorship was devised where members were assigned discipling partners. While some have blamed strict and, often, oppressive structure for problems that were experienced, I believe the problem is more fundamental. Under the banner of discipling, a potpourri of scriptural commands and principles were stirred together into one pot. In so doing, the final product strayed from the spirit of God's word and the focus of the relationships shifted from the Bible's intent. The structure compounded the problem, but the misrepresentation of scripture was at the root. There are a couple of basic areas where the scriptures differ from what was practiced by the discipling movement.

The Definition of Discipling:

In English, the term discipling is not a "real" word. Disciple is not a verb. The reason why we use the term discipling is because in the original language of the New Testament, Koine Greek, disciple is used as a verb. In fact, it is used as a verb four times (Acts 14:21, Matt13:52, Matt 27:57, and Matt 28:19). Because discipling is a real Bible word, it is imperative that we define it the way the Bible does and practice it the way that the scriptures intended.

The Greek word translated to disciple is matheteuo. A more complete definition of matheteuo is: "To be or to make to be a disciple, to disciple to make a disciple to train as a follower, instruct as an adherent, mentor. The action of the verb describes much more than academic impartation of information, it suggests the shaping of character and the cultivation of a world-view through a close, personal relationship between student and teacher" *[Definition taken from The Hebrew-Greek Key Word Study Bible page 1647]*.

Matthew 28:19, the great commission, is the only one of the four verses using matheteuo which truly qualifies as a command.   In this verse, we are told to go and matheteuo all nations (to train, to mold, to mentor, to disciple) and after we have discipled them, to baptize them. It is a specific command from the Lord, given to the apostles and passed on to us. The second part is like it.   After the person is baptized, we are commanded to teach him to obey everything that Jesus commanded. So, Jesus commands us to disciple non-Christians in preparation for baptism and to disciple young Christians to maturity. What do we learn from this passage? We learn that discipling is biblical; it is commanded, and it is an essential aspect of our relationships with one another in God's church. We ignore this command at our risk, and there will be something missing from our fellowships until it is completely and accurately obeyed.

A true discipling relationship is a teacher/student relationship. It involves mentoring someone and helping to instruct and mold character.   What is described here is not a one another relationship rather it is a relationship between an instructor and an apprentice. Using the term discipling as a synonym for the one another commands is a misuse of the term. Discipling is a unique relationship, a specific and necessary means of accomplishing the meeting of specific needs in the church, needs that cannot be met any other way.

While it is important, it is essential to understand that discipling is a small aspect of Christian interaction. One another relationships are the relationships that all disciples are commanded to have. One another relationships are necessary for every stage and in every aspect of the Christian life. There are countless directives given by the Spirit for us describing what we are to be for each other. No one is too mature in Christ to need them or too young or weak in the Lord to have something to offer. One another relationships are what define the body of Christ. They are the muscles and tendons that hold the body of Christ together. Still, disicpling relationships play a narrow but valuable role. There are five major needs that discipling meets.

1. It is the Bible's way of training preachers and prophets
2. It is the way of equipping and raising up leaders
3. It is the way to convert non-Christians

4. It is the way of shepherding, equipping, and maturing baby Christians

5. It is a way of imparting specific knowledge or skills.

Even though the term matheteuo only appears in the New Testament four times, the principle can be seen throughout the Bible. It is how Moses raised up Joshua and how Elijah trained Elisha. We see it at work in the relationship of Paul and Timothy and most importantly we see that it was the method used by Jesus for molding His apostles. Discipling is certainly part of God's plan for His people. The problem with the discipling movement is that it was poorly defined and poorly applied. There are three fundamental mistakes made by the discipling movement concerning discipling and one another relationships.

1. Wrong Emphasis
2. Wrong Plan
3. Wrong Model

Wrong Emphasis

In the Bible, the emphasis of Christian relationships is overwhelmingly one another relationships, Christians helping each other, not as teacher student, but brother to brother. In the discipling movement, the term discipling was used as a synonym for one another relationships and the charge to disciple, in theory, encompassed a charge to obey all of the one another passages. The Discipling Movement was supposed to have been the One Another Movement. Although this was the theory, this is not what transpired.

The truth of it is that the Discipling Movement became The Mentoring Movement. Every member was assigned a discipling partner, charged with the goal of mentoring and training him or her. Their "discipler" was over them in the Lord. He was the teacher; the "disciplee" was the student. It created a pyramid, with the congregational leader at the top, which always begged the question, "Who discipled the man at the top?"

No matter how long someone was in the Lord, no matter what his level of maturity, he was always someone's apprentice, a permanent student. Now, no one would ever argue that all disciples need to be humble and need to remain learners throughout their Christian walk, but the charge to learn from one another is very different than having someone specifically assigned over you. One taught and the other learned. One confessed his sins and the other listened. Rather than fostering one another relationships, it suffocated them, creating levels of pride and hierarchy much deeper than any system. In many cases, this relational dysfunction still endures long after the structure was eventually dissolved.

Not surprisingly, the tiered mentoring worked well when applied to baby Christians, was very effective in training young leaders, and was equally effective in providing guidance for new preachers. Most others struggled. It strained friendships, capped faith, fostered false authority, lent itself to harshness, stunted spiritual growth, and created unhealthy dependency. Worse, it buried the one another passages under a mountain of pride and structure. The "discipling tree" inhibited the natural growth of Christian relationships and made peer relationships rare when they are the primary relationships of scripture. The effect of being assigned a "discipler" when someone had been in the Lord, ten, fifteen, or twenty years was humiliating and the idea that a mature evangelist, with ten, twenty or thirty years experience, still needed an overseeing evangelist was emasculating.

There is no question that every disciple, no matter what his level of maturity, needs people in his or her life. I am not against prayer partners, discipling partners, or any other partnership between mature disciples if the relationship is indeed a partnership. In fact such partnerships are absolutely necessary. We all have a need for intimate, powerful spiritual relationships, but the bulk of these relationships are designed to be reciprocal. The Spirit did not write so many one another passages without purpose. One another, is the language of love, the language of family. It should be the nature of all mature relationships in the Lord. When the Discipling Movement" became the One Over Each Other Movement" rather than "The One Another Movement", it lost its way. The intentions were good and much good was done, but the wrong emphasis created a myriad of problems and some bad habits that have proved difficult to break.

Wrong Plan

Let me repeat, having said all this, there is a place for discipling, discipling in the pure teacher student sense of the word. The five areas listed earlier cannot be successfully done without it:

1. It is the Bible's way of training preachers and prophets
2. It is the way of equipping and raising up leaders
3. It is the way to convert non-Christians
4. It is the way of shepherding, equipping, and maturing baby Christians
5. It is a way of imparting specific knowledge or skills.

We will delve into more detail about the nature of discipling in later chapters. For now, suffice it to say that part of the problem of how it was done in the Discipling Movement was the way it was structured, specifically the duration. In the Bible, discipling is temporary. The teacher apprentice relationship is a short-term relationship until the student reaches maturity. Elijah trained Elisha then moved on. Timothy, Paul's timid apprentice, grew up and was sent out on his own, changing the nature of their relationship. Saul (who became the apostle Paul) started out as Barnabas' apprentice (Acts 11:22-26) but grew to become his partner in the gospel. Even, the apostles graduated, as flawed as they were, going from Jesus students to his friends in three years (John 15:9-17). Yes, I understand that they still were Jesus' disciples. We all are Jesus' disciples for life but their training by Him in the ministry was short term. After three years, they were sent out. They had graduated. This is the Lord's way.

In the Bible, discipling is a temporary method of equipping. The young Christian quickly grows from student to brother, the young preacher grows from apprentice to partner, to peer. This is the natural order of things. No one was meant to be an apprentice forever. It is unhealthy, a type of co-dependency that cripples both teacher and student, creating pride and insecurity, instruction and shallowness, resentment and reliance.

Maturity cannot be dangled as a carrot, like some unattainable prize. Is the teacher mature, flawed, as he is, sinful as he is? If such a fallible servant can be considered to have some mastery of the basics, maturity cannot be that difficult to attain. None of us has that much to teach. The idea that someone requires a lifetime learning what we know is sheer arrogance. God, please forgive me for such arrogance. We do not know that much and even the one teacher who knew all things finished his discipling of the leaders for God's kingdom on earth in three years. They graduated from having a teacher to only having each other. They went from a discipling relationship to the one another way. That is God's plan. Discipling is a conduit to one another relationships. We were meant to teach each other; correct each other, serve each other, admonish each other, and encourage each other. Helping the student to get to that point as quickly as possible is the goal of a discipling relationship. We do not need mentors for life, but we need brothers and sisters for eternity.

Wrong Model

There were two primary problems with the model the Discipling Movement used for discipling: We did not follow Jesus' example enough and we imitated parts of Jesus' example that are not meant to be imitated.

We were in such a rush to baptize that we did not invest enough in training. Adequate time was not spent with young Christians or young leaders and for young Christians, the time spent was often spent with the least qualified people in the church. The result is that young Christians often never matured and young leaders were often given responsibility well beyond their levels of faith and wisdom. Jesus invested in his disciples. Time, energy, love, he invested everything. He taught them scriptures; he taught them principles; he taught them how to pray; how to love and how to share their faith. The apostles were able to graduate in three years because for three years they had the Lord's full attention. They were forever changed.

We cut corners. We were so busy trying to convert the next person that baby Christians were discipled in name only. Levels of spiritual maturity that should have been attained in months took years or were never reached at all. To compensate, people were spoon fed and led along by small group leaders who often ended up functioning as spiritual baby sitters. Instead of taking time to help each member develop deep convictions, systems of accountability were created to keep the church "in check". The structure was developed to fix a problem. The structure didn't fix the problem; it compounded it, but getting rid of the structure didn't address the problem either. What was the problem? Disciples were not maturing.

Why? We were too busy adding souls to actually build God's church. We were not investing in maturing the flock and training leaders who were truly equipped to shepherd and lead powerfully in the kingdom. The faster we went, the more corners we cut, the less we grew. We built on Christ's foundation with straw not precious stones and when the time of testing came, too many souls were blown away.

Jesus invested. He could have spent three years attempting to win the maximum number of souls. Instead, he spent three years investing in the ones he had. The result: After he ascended, His students became mighty leaders of God's kingdom, and under their leadership, the church evangelized the known world during their lifetime. We should have paid closer attention to Christ's example.

The other problem is that we attempted to imitate parts of Christ's example that were not meant for us. How is that possible? Christ, through His word left us a myriad of one another commands (commands not suggestions). Yet, He did not practice them. We are told to confess our sins to one another (again this is a command not a suggestion), but Christ never confessed His sins. We are told to teach one another, to correct one another, and even to rebuke each other, but Christ never allowed any of His disciples to teach correct, or rebuke

Him (Peter tried to rebuke Jesus Matthew 16:21-23 but that didn't turn out too well). Jesus did not practice many of the one another principles. Why? He is perfect. He is always right, always pure, always holy, and always humble. Of course, Peter confessed his sins to Jesus but Jesus did not reciprocate. Jesus pointed out James's shortcomings, but James was not allowed to question Jesus. Jesus was always the teacher and never truly a peer. One another scriptures were not for Him; they are for us.

Jesus' interaction with the apostles was purely teacher student and rightfully so, but we cannot insert ourselves in place of Jesus and have the same interaction with our students that Jesus had with His. We are flawed. He was not. Even in our discipling relationships, we always need a one another component because in our case, the apprentice is being mentored by a sinner.

More often than not, the discipling movement imitated Jesus' model to a fault. The discipler assumed the role of Jesus. He was always the teacher, always the expert in every area. The disciplee confessed sins to him, rarely the other way around. The disciplee sought advice. The discipler gave advice. If the teacher had something to confess or needed help, he talked to someone "above" him, if there was someone. For his student, he was always the teacher, never a peer. The flaw with this is obvious. We are not Jesus. We are not perfect, not experts in every area, not always righteous, not always pure. We have strengths and weaknesses, having the need to learn from even those we are teaching. Even the weakest among us has strengths that others do not have, and even the wisest among us, cannot see himself clearly. We need others to point out our faults. This method of discipling ignored these realities and created an illusion that ultimately damaged both teacher and student.

To paraphrase an old commercial, the goal of the discipler was to never let a disciple see him sweat. The reasons why this type of discipling was unhealthy are nearly too numerous to list. Ironically, the ones that suffered the most from this approach were the teachers, particularly those at the top of the discipling tree. Such an approach fostered extreme pride and hierarchy and made it incredibly difficult for members to develop, healthy reciprocal friendships. So, how did the leader at the top of the tree get spiritual help? He did not consider his disciples his peers, had never built relationships based on humility and mutual respect. Sadly, the leaders with the most responsibility, who dished out spiritual counsel the most, were the ones who got little or no direction for their own lives and had built up thick walls of pride that made it difficult to be approached. The experienced leaders, that they discipled but to whom they rarely listened, were often frustrated, even resentful creating a recipe for disaster. Honest criticism of the top discipler was rarely rewarded and often a bad career move, creating an environment similar to the children's story, "The Emperor's New Clothes". In the tale, believing that he had purchased a marvelous new outfit, the emperor walked around naked. The sycophants around him were too intimidated to tell him the truth, so they told him only what he wanted to hear. This is a deadly environment, poison for all involved, destroying the very fabric of what should be sacred in Christian interaction.

There is a practical example that I think illustrates the old dynamic within the "Discipling Movement". In the mid-nineties, a preacher who had been in the ministry for eleven years, and his wife moved to a major city to serve a mega-congregation with a large ministry staff. A mature ministry couple was assigned to disciple them. The young couple was going through a rocky time in their marriage and the older couple offered invaluable help. They taught their younger counterparts principles that quickly turned their marriage around, principles that the younger couple still relies on to this day. There is no question, that the new couple needed the mature couples' mentoring in the areas of marriage and parenting, but even back then, there were other areas where the younger pair could have helped them, strengths that they had that were not necessarily strengths of the more established duo.

That wasn't the nature of the relationship. The new couple confessed sin; the other listened. The new couple received solicited and unsolicited advice in areas of weakness and strength and the mature couple gave advice about areas where they were strong and areas where they were not. Even though the younger preacher and his wife saw cracks in their friends (all of us have cracks), the older couple did not share their struggles with their disciples and the younger couple was not free to share what they saw.

After the two couples had been friends over seven years, long after the younger couple's marriage had turned around, the dynamic of the relationship still had never changed. During this period, the church went through a difficult time, the church leaders who discipled the older couple, crashed spiritually, and the older couple was struggling badly. The younger couple wanted to help, to talk to them, but the mature pair wouldn't, they couldn't be open with their younger co-workers. That's not how it worked. They helped their disciples; their disciples did not help them. The younger couple saw their friends drown spiritually, slaves of a flawed model; even after the discipling structure itself was abandoned, they were enslaved by thirty years of a very bad habit.

There are too many stories like this from the old Discipling Movement and for too many years, I was as guilty as anyone of hurting people through arrogant discipling. Even now, far too many disciples, particularly veteran preachers, find it hard to build peer relationships and nearly impossible to accept spiritual help from people that they had formerly been "over" in the Lord.   Long after the system of discipling trees have been disassembled, they are prisoners of pride, never having learned the skills necessary to have successful peer friendships, particularly with their former disciples. Many only know how to have vertical relationships. Once we have dared to sit in Jesus' seat, it is difficult to step down.

Does this mean that discipling is wrong? Does it mean that it is impossible to have successful teacher student relationships in the church? No!   Healthy discipling is possible and necessary. We simply need to imitate many of Jesus' principles while remembering that we are not Jesus. We are not only the teacher. Our first relationship with any disciple is that of brother or sister.   That relationship supercedes all others because we stand on equal ground before the cross. Even as a mentor helps a young Christian with Christian basics, he must remember that they are brothers before they are anything else, and they must be willing to respect each other as brothers and

help each other as such apart from their student teacher
relationship.

Suppose I went to work in a company where my physical
brother was a supervisor, working a job where I had no previous
experience. On the job, my brother would be my mentor, it's
not two way learning; he's the teacher, my boss; I'm the student.
Off the job, that dynamic goes out the door. We're just
brothers, free to have fun, help each other, disagree, and even
fight. He wouldn't act as my boss in every area and he's not the
expert in every area. While I would defer to his expertise at
work, after five, we're just brothers and that is the far more
important, more lasting dynamic.

I was hired by a mega-church in New York City in May of 2004
and took over a region of the congregation based in Brooklyn.
There was a young couple on staff that had obvious holes in
their training and my wife and I were charged with filling those
holes. In one of my first conversations with the young preacher
I told him that we were going to have two distinct relationships.
The first relationship is as brothers. I respected him as a man
and as a brother. I needed and wanted a strong one another
relationship where he felt free to talk to me about any
weaknesses that he saw in my marriage, my family, and me and
I would do the same for him. I told him that long after we

finished working together we were going to be friends and brothers. This is our most important relationship. Then I said that our second relationship is the ministry. My job is to train him and at this point of his development, I needed to be the teacher and he needed to be the student. Now, my goal is to equip him so that we could function as peers and partners in the ministry as soon as possible, but until he'd mastered the basics, he needed to have the humility to be an apprentice in this area. There were other areas where he could teach me, and at some point he'd be seasoned enough that we could help each other in ministry, but at this time, that was not where he was. My job was to get him there.

That is the paraphrased version of the conversation, and it is what I believed then and still believe the spirit of discipling needs to be. By the way, my relationship with this young preacher went great. He and his wife have gone on to do exceptional work in the ministry and remain some of our closest friends. Yes, we need teacher student relationships, but we must remember that they are temporary, they must evolve, and that we are brothers first.

Conclusion

We must learn from our failures and hold more accurately to the biblical model. The remainder of this book is an attempt to accomplish this. One another relationships are the lifeblood of the church. Disicpling is an important tool in church building. This book is dedicated to outlining how we can truly live out God's plan for both. We cannot simply repeat past mistakes or become jaded and cease our attempts to live out these principles. The church will never be whole until we have successfully restored these practices. I am grateful for what has come before, the good and the bad. Through Christ it will lay a foundation for a glorious future.

No Other Way

For all the mistakes that have been made by churches that have tried to practice discipling and one another relationships, the biggest mistake is not vigorously attempting to put these scriptures into practice. The church is Christ's bride, His body. If we stray from the blueprint He has laid out for it, we do so at our own peril. We can never ignore God's commands without consequence. So much of the weakness found in modern Christianity can be traced to the lack of adherence to these passages. For those of us who have sought to practice the one another way and to forge discipling relationships it will be to our shame, if we let past failures and hurts make us waver in our commitment to both. For congregations to mature and experience dynamic growth and revival, we must have a revival in helping every disciple commit to intimate spiritual friendships. We can accept no substitutes, for there is no other way.

End The Uncertainty

Many disciples are confused. So much has been said and written about discipling in the last few years, much of it conflicting. More than a few articles have been posted on the Internet, stemming more from emotion than from thorough study of scripture. I frequently talk to Christians who say discipling isn't Biblical or they are confused about past practices concerning what is scripture and what was structure. Between the sting of past hurts and the fog of uncertainty, too many have retreated, becoming isolated, coming to services but not connected. The type of relationships that God desires cannot be achieved without commitment and an investment in each other. It is far more than casual friendship. We must have strong clear teaching about the one another way, to cut through the confusion and challenge every disciple to get off the fence and invest in a few spiritual friendships.

Accept No Substitutions

The needs that are met by obedience to the one another passages cannot be met any other way. We need strong, balanced Biblical preaching and teaching, but the pulpit alone will never make a church healthy. At some point, every disciple needs the personal touch, the personal connection. I've made a few decisions to change while sitting in a sermon, but most of my life-changing decisions have come in a one on one conversation with a close friend and an open Bible. Most of the miracles I've seen in the lives of others, drug addicts getting clean, marriages on the verge of divorce turning around, men addicted to impurity and immorality breaking free, have happened during one on one interactions or in small group sessions, where there were a few good brothers or sisters who loved each other, the Holy Spirit, and the word. No sermon, or class by itself would ever have achieved this. It is the power of the one another way, in all of its glory.

As our commitment to the one another way has lessoned, we have seen a severe decrease in miracles as well as a sharp increase in blatant sin, failed marriages and lukewarm commitment. This is no coincidence. We will never disregard God's commands without consequence. When we recommit to God's plan for our fellowship, the miracles will return.

God's way is the only way. Young Christian classes are great, but they cannot replace Matthew 28:19. Young Christians need the personal touch; they need a mentor and a friend. Marriage classes are a wonderful idea, but they cannot replace the personal interaction of two couples getting together consistently and faithfully encouraging one another, serving one another, loving one another, admonishing one another, and when necessary rebuking one another. I am all for preachers sitting in classes and getting theological training if it is in addition to the training that Barnabas gave Paul, that Paul gave Timothy, and that Jesus gave the apostles. We must walk with the wise to become wise (Proverbs 13:20). Discipling is the Lord's method of training preachers. We can add to that training, but it is our folly if we seek to replace it or diminish its importance.

God's thoughts are not our thoughts neither are His ways our ways (Isaiah 55:8-10). We must seek to understand and apply the wisdom of God and not lean on our own understanding. Truthfully, we need to obey the Lord whether or not we understand why. His foolishness will be more effective than our wisdom. We have no option but to restore discipling and the one another way. If we fail, our churches will fail. If we waver, our faith will waver. God's plan is perfect. Let us walk His walk and let Him lead us to glory. There is no other way.

The One Another Way

For the rest of this book we are going to separate the discussion of discipling and the one another way, defining one another relationships as relationships that are primarily reciprocal and discipling relationships as relationships that are primarily mentoring in nature. From my perspective, the one another passages are the lifeblood of the church, while discipling functions as an irreplaceable church building tool. Chapters four through eight focus on the one another passages and their practical application while chapters nine and ten focus on discipling.

Philippians 4:8 states, *"Finally, brothers, whatever is true, whatever is noble, whatever is right, whatever is pure, whatever is lovely, whatever is admirable-if anything is excellent or praiseworthy-think about such things."*

In thinking back over my time in the church, I've tried to focus, particularly on the good times, the times I saw miracles, the times I felt unimaginable love, the things that worked. Where there is joy, love, and a demonstration of God's power then surely this is an example of a command or spiritual principle at work, either because we consciously obeyed or simply stumbled upon it. Where there is pain, hurt, and division this is generally an example of us missing the mark. Our goal must be to imitate the good while sifting out the junk. I think we can learn a lot if we can answer the question, "What made the good times good?"

I remember very fondly my time as a young disciple in our congregation's campus ministry at the University of Maryland (Go Terps!). Our campus ministry consisted of approximately one hundred students from both the University of Maryland and Howard University with John Brush serving as the campus minister. It was fun, it was fruitful, and it was family. We were part of the Discipling Movement but we existed on the outskirts (sort of like the movement equivalent of Luke Skywalker's home planet from the Star Wars Trilogies, Tatooine). During the years I was involved, from 1983 to 1986, our ministry was far enough removed from Gainesville and Boston, the "epicenters" of the Discipling Movement, that much of the legalism and control that had already begun to permeate some other

ministries was lost on us. At that time, we were largely oblivious
to it, just having fun, trying to graduate, love one another, and
win the world for Jesus.

We embraced the one another way, often without even
completely understanding what we were doing. We prayed
together, hung out together, learned from each other,
exchanged advice, confessed sin, corrected each other, laughed
together, and even cried together. We took care of each other,
put up with each other, and took in one another when the
financial aid didn't come in as expected. We weren't being
inspired by discipling trees and there was no one standing over
our heads telling us what to do, no stats being kept to motivate
us, and no benevolence committee holding us accountable for
meeting needs. We simply loved each other. It was personal; it
was intimate; it was powerful. We would have died for each
other and praised God for the opportunity to do so.

We didn't know to be motivated by anything else. We seriously
believed that there was nothing more important than going to
heaven and bringing as many souls with us as we could. We
were deeply committed to walking in Jesus' steps, including
being celibate until marriage, resisting lust and pornography,
commitment to the body, excellence in our academic examples,
saying no to drunkenness and illegal drugs, and spreading the

message of the gospel. At Maryland there were over 37,000 undergraduate students. There were only about sixty of us. We lived in the dorms or in off campus apartment complexes. All around us students were sleeping around. The dorm room walls were plastered with pornographic images. There were keg parties Thursday through Sunday and orgies a few rooms down on a fairly frequent basis. A girl I knew was date raped down the hall. It wasn't called date rape back then and it was fairly common. Back then the date rape drug was alcohol. Guys bragged about it, exchanging tips on the best way to do it. The unmistakable smell of weed filled the air every night and cocaine was being used in someone's room virtually every weekend. Disciples had to contend daily with half-naked co-eds and our own raging hormones. And of course, there was persecution. Guys, who were celibate, didn't get drunk, go to wild parties, or yell catcalls at women were called Jesus freaks or worse. It was just part of the cost of being a disciple.

We quickly figured out that we needed each other. If we were serious about this, if we really believed that radical commitment to Jesus was the only way, we knew that the only way for any of us to make it to heaven was for all of us to lean heavily on each other. I needed to pray, I needed to read my Bible, daily, more than daily, and I needed my brothers and sisters. I needed other disciples, not like I needed a Big Mac; I needed them like

I needed air. We became best friends, inseparable, because we knew we wouldn't stay faithful to the narrow road any other way.

So when I was struggling with lustful thoughts, I teamed up with a brother and we talked, encouraged each other, prayed together, memorized scriptures, spurred each other on, confessed temptation and shared victories daily. When I was going through a hard time with my dad, my friends showed up unannounced, gathered around, opened their Bibles, challenged me to forgive, and prayed with me until the tears streamed down my face. When one of the sisters was kicked out of her parents' house and cut off, we rushed around her prayed with her, and sisters moved her into their place and even helped her with her finances. When I was totally broke and couldn't afford food, some sisters found out about it, and completely on their own, showed up at my dorm room and stocked my shelves with groceries. When a good friend of mine fell into sexual immorality, I showed up at his door, opened my Bible, rebuked him, encouraged him, and stayed and prayed long into the night. No one told us to do these things. We didn't really have a system. We were compelled by love, by need, and friendship that was much deeper than friendship. We had become family.

This kind of love is powerful. I had never considered myself prejudiced. I had always grown up in integrated environments and had friends from different races. I hung out with all kinds of people, so I figured I was immune. Now, I didn't date other races, and I wasn't in favor of interracial dating in general, even going so far as to write an article for the school paper about my feelings regarding the subject during my freshman year, but in my mind, that wasn't prejudice, it was racial pride and practical thinking. As you can see, self-deception was one of my strong points.

On Maryland's campus there was a fair amount of racial tension. Races hung out but it had limits, invisible barriers that weren't crossed. It was always interesting going from the dorms to the dining hall. Everyone would be laughing and hanging out, (black, white, whatever) but when we actually got inside, all the whites would sit at tables together and all the blacks would sit separately, with very few exceptions. The disciples were a big exception. They would sit together, a regular rainbow coalition. Not only that, they did everything together, with no barriers. They hung out at church; they hung out all over campus; they took each other home and visited each other's parents; they dated; they even fell in love.   Initially, I was skeptical, but as I got to know them, I saw that these students were truly color blind, probably, the first truly color blind

people I had ever met.   Later on I discovered that this fact
created some tension between the students and the adults at
church, even those with similar convictions about discipleship,
but that is a story for another time. The point is the students let
Christ bring them together in a way I had never seen.   It
convicted me, exposing the racism in my own heart. I saw the
barriers of distrust I had erected, the limits I had put on my
friendships, the racist limits I'd put on love. Without a sermon,
without a conversation, simply the example of one another love
changed my life, flushed out my sin, and forced me to repent. I
opened my heart to trust without limit, care without limit, and
to love without limit. We were no color except red, colored by
the blood of Christ. Love taught me this, screaming louder than
any sermon, cleansing me, washing me in its glow.

Why do I share all of this? Because way back then in that little
campus ministry, that was where I got my first taste of the
power of one another love. It was only a taste, raw and
unpolluted by either man made rules and systems or the jaded
cynicism that often comes with "spiritual maturity". But that
taste convinces me that if we dare to believe, believe with that
same idealistic fervor of naïve college students, the one another
way will change our lives.

John 13:34-35 Is the ultimate one another scripture, stating, *"A new command I give you: Love one another. As I have loved you, so you must love one another. By this all men will know that you are my disciples, if you love one another."*

We could spend a lifetime gleaming lessons from this one scripture; yet, there are a few fundamental lessons that leap out at us. First, loving one another in this way is a mark of discipleship, a large part of what sets Jesus' disciples apart from the rest of the world. Displaying this supernatural love is what makes us stand out, shining like a light on a hill. This love is truly supernatural, so only through depending on the Spirit do we have hope of obeying this command. Jesus instructs His church to love each other the way that He loves us. This means that our love for each other must be unconditional. It is not based on what someone has done for us or whether he/she reciprocates. We do not serve only our friends or disciples that we know personally. We extend this love to all of our brothers and sisters, free of charge with no strings attached. Jesus' love is color blind, culture blind, appearance blind, and class blind. Jesus loves without limit, laying down His life for us. Likewise, he calls us to lay down our lives for our brothers and sisters (I John 3:16). Jesus loves intimately. He does not love from a distance. We need to build intimate relationships in the body of Christ. I believe that all the one another passages in the Bible, the ones that use the phrase one another and the ones that describe this concept with different terminology, are designed to help us to understand how to love each other the way Jesus loves us.   He breaks it down piece-by-piece, scripture by scripture, not leaving it up to our own imaginations.   When we truly put these passages into practice, personally and in our churches, it will unleash the power of Christ's love like never before.

Below is a sampling of some of the one another commands from the scriptures:

(*Please, take a few minutes to study these scriptures.   Everything written in the next few chapters is based on the commands and principles from these passages.)

A.   Colossians 3: 16: "Let the word of Christ dwell in you richly as you teach and admonish one another with all wisdom, and as you sing psalms, hymns and spiritual songs with gratitude in your hearts to God." This passage commands us to admonish one another. This is a word that doesn't get used very often in every day speech. Although preachers use the word admonish in their sermons from time to time, most members (and many preachers) have no idea about the true meaning of the word so we don't truly understand the nature of this command. The word translated admonish in this passage comes from the Greek word Noutheteo: Meaning to Teach and Admonish (to rebuke mildly, advise strongly-to warn someone of their error, alert them to the consequences of their error, and to show them the means of correcting their problem) This is a weighty command, a command that can only truly be obeyed among individuals committed to having intimate spiritual friendships. **{Definition taken The Hebrew-Greek Key Word Study Bible page 1654}**

B. James 5: 16: *"Therefore confess your sins to each other and pray for each other so that you may be healed. The prayer of a righteous man is powerful and effective."* This verse commands us to confess our sins to one another and to pray for each other. Confessing our sins to each other so we can help and pray for each other is a command from God not a request. Just confessing our sins to God is not enough. He desires that we confess to one another.

C. Galatians 5: 13: *"You, my brothers, were called to be free. But do not use your freedom to indulge the sinful nature; rather, serve one another in love"* We are commanded us to serve one another. The Greek word translated serve here is Douleuo (which means to be a slave, stand as a slave to another). God has bound us to each other, compelling us by Christ's love to serve each other. **{*Definition taken The Hebrew-Greek Key Word Study Bible page 1611*}**

D.   *1 Thessalonians 5: 11*: *"Therefore encourage one another and build each other up, just as in fact you are doing."* We are commanded to encourage one another.

E. *Heb 3:13*: *"But encourage one another daily, as long as it is called Today, so that none of you may be hardened by sin's deceitfulness."* This passage takes it a step further commanding us to encourage one another daily. There is nothing that we need more from our brothers and sisters than encouragement.

F. *Hebrews 10: 24*: *"And let us consider how we may spur one another on toward love and good deeds."* We are told to consider how we can spur one another on toward love and good deeds.   This is more than just the responsibility of the evangelists and elders. We all have a responsibility to spur on our brothers and sisters.

G. Colossians 3: 13: *"Bear with each other and forgive whatever grievances you may have against one another. Forgive as the Lord forgave you"* We are commanded to forgive one another. We all need grace because messing up is what we do best. We need to extend grace to each other.

H. Ephesians 4: 2: *"Be completely humble and gentle; be patient, bearing with one another in love."* This scripture commands us to be patient with one another. This passage is tailor made for husbands and wives…roommates too.

I. Ephesians 4: 32: *"Be kind and compassionate to one another, forgiving each other, just as in Christ God forgave you."* We are commanded to have compassion for one another. We need empathy for others' circumstances, and to understand that meeting needs in the church is not just the responsibility of leadership or a specific ministry. It is all of our responsibility.

J. Ephesians 5: 21: *"Submit to one another out of reverence for Christ."* Commands us to submit to one other. Humility has great healing power.

K. Romans 12:16 *Live in harmony with one another. Do not be proud, but be willing to associate with people of low position. Do not be conceited."* Commands us to live in harmony with one another.

L. Romans 12:10*: "Be devoted to one another in brotherly love. Honor one another above yourselves."* Commands us to honor one another above ourselves. Too often, I am my own favorite person. This is a powerful, challenging scripture.

M. Romans 12:10*: "Be devoted to one another in brotherly love. Honor one another above yourselves."* Commands us to be devoted to one another. Without devotion it is impossible to build family.

N. Romans 15:7*: "Accept one another, then, just as Christ accepted you, in order to bring praise to God."* Commands us to accept one another as Christ accepted us. We are all fruits and nuts with our own quirks and foibles and lots of baggage. In addition, we come from different generations, different races, different economic groups, different cultures, and even different corners of the earth. There is great power in this passage.

O.   Proverbs 27:17*:   "As iron sharpens iron, so one man sharpens another."*

P.   Proverbs 18:24*: "A man of many companions may come to ruin, but there is a friend who sticks closer than a brother."*

Q.   Proverbs 17:17*:   " A friend loves at all times, and a brother is born for adversity."*

R.   Proverbs 15:22*: "Plans fail for lack of counsel, but with many advisers they succeed."*

S.   Ephesians 4: 15-16: *"Instead, speaking the truth in love, we will in all things grow up into him who is the Head, that is, Christ. From him the whole body, joined and held together by every supporting ligament, grows and builds itself up in love, as each part does its work."* This passage encourages us to speak the truth in love to one another. Too often the truth is rare and truth speakers are an endangered species.

T.   I Peter 4:8*: "Love each other deeply, because love covers over a multitude of sins."* **I Peter 1:22** is a sister passage.

These passages present a road map, designed to take us to an amazing destination while traveling down a narrow road. Come; let us continue our journey, following in the footsteps of

Jesus every step of the way. I am sure He will make it worth our while.

The Heart of the Matter

The one another passages are inspiring, motivating, and extremely challenging, but what do they mean practically? How do we apply them to our everyday Christian walk? The practical application involves investing in deep spiritual friendships.

> **Ecclesiastes 4:9-12** *"Two are better than one, because they have a good return for their work: If one falls down his friend can help him up. But pity the man who falls and has no one to help him! Also, if two lie down together, they will keep warm. But how can one keep warm alone? Though one may be overpowered, two can defend themselves. A cord of three strands is not quickly broken."*

We are not meant to make it on our own. Obviously, we are meant to depend on God through Christ, but part of being connected to Christ is being connected to Christ's body. The church is the body of Christ, making Christianity the ultimate team sport. The older we get, often the more guarded and independent we become, but as life gets more complex, the spiritual stakes get higher and the necessity for a spiritual support system increases, not decreases. The truth is, many of the one another passages express a love and concern that we need for all believers. Other commands are commands that can only be fully obeyed when there is a level of intimacy to our relationships. James 5:16 commands us to confess our sins to one another. Do you want to confess your sins to a stranger or a casual acquaintance? Do you want to confess to someone with whom you have not built trust or who does not trust you enough to be open with you? In Colossians 3:16, the Bible commands us to admonish one another. Remember admonishment means to rebuke mildly, advise strongly-to warn someone of their error, alert them to the consequences of their error, and to show them the means of correcting their problem. Do you want to give that type of counsel to a casual acquaintance or accept it from someone with whom there is little or no emotional connection? Unless there is depth in our Christian friendships, these types of passages will not be obeyed and if they are, without the depth, attempts at obedience will be awkward and legalistic.

Proverbs 18:24 states, *"A man of many companions will come to ruin but there is a friend who is closer than a brother."*

This is the heart of the matter. As disciples we have many companions, all sorts of Christian friends and acquaintances, but unless we have a friend who is closer than a brother, we are spiritually at risk. It is great to have more than one, but we all need at least one. We are not going to have a lot, even in God's kingdom. Now, I am not saying that we cannot have a large number of friendships. Of course we can. We can and should have many companions with varied degrees of closeness. But a Proverbs 18:24 friendship is special, it is essential, and it is rare. Sometimes disciples have unrealistic expectations and expect to be super close to almost everyone and are hurt when it does not happen. The truth is, if we are fortunate, really fortunate, God will bless us with two or three of these special brothers and sisters. Jesus had numerous friends and followers. He had twelve apostles and I'm sure he was close to all of them, but in the end he only had three best friends, James, Peter, and John. If even Jesus, who was perfect, focused on a few, what does that say about you and me?

Proverbs 27:17 states, *" As iron sharpens iron so one man sharpens another."*

The other quality of these special friendships is spirituality. The goal is not just to have a few close friendships but also to have these friendships with men and women whose goal is to help you make it to heaven.   The goal of the relationship is to sharpen each other spiritually, to make each other better for God. II Corinthians 6:14-20 warns us not to be unevenly yoked with unbelievers. What does this mean? It means that we can have all sorts of friendships with saved and unsaved alike, but our closest relationships, the ones that have the most spiritual influence on us, need to be with disciples who are strong in the Lord.   If your most intimate relationships are with people who are lost or disciples who are not committed, you have put yourself spiritually at risk. It takes iron to sharpen iron.

This principle applies to platonic friendships, but surely it applies to romantic relationships as well. No one will have more influence on you spiritually, than the one you love. If being in love does not constitute a yoke, then yokes do not exist. The person to whom you are attracted, the one you are dating is he or she a disciple? If so, is he doing well spiritually? If not, how can someone sharpen you spiritually, if he or she is not right with God himself. Is your relationship based on Proverbs 27:17, with the goal being to help each other be stronger for Jesus? If not, why are you together? Has your zeal, your passion, your fruitfulness for God increased since you have been together or decreased. **I Corinthians 15:33 says,** *"Do not be misled: Bad company corrupts good character."* Who you decide to love is the second most important decision of your life; only your decision to follow Jesus is greater. Why is it so important? Because that bond will either sharpen you or corrupt you. The one you are dating, how do you know whether God has sent him or Satan has sent him to lure you away? Has the relationship influenced you to pray or lead you into impurity? Spiritual love will build up your faith not tear it down. This is free bonus material because this is not a book on dating, but if you are single, wait on God. Don't you dare compromise and yoke your heart to someone who is not a disciple, placing your trust in someone who has not placed his trust in Jesus. And don't give your heart to just any disciple because more important than their looks, their money, or their race is the sincerity of their faith. Will loving them improve your chances of going to heaven? If the answer is no, wait; wait on God. "As iron sharpens irons so one man sharpens another." Never settle for less.

O.K., that's it for the bonus material. Now, that I've gotten that out of my system, let's get back to our primary topic, Proverbs 18:24 friendships, a spiritual friend who is closer than a brother. We need them, but these types of friendships are not easy and do not come naturally. Having this kind of bond takes investment. We must make an investment of time and emotion. Just going to church, having some buddies, checking out the game isn't going to do it. If we invest in everyone, that is the equivalent of investing in no one, or to quote the movie "The Incredibles", " If everyone is special then nobody is." We have to focus on a few, or for starters maybe even the one, and devote time to forging a spiritual bond a special bond. I'm talking about a bond where you trust each other, you can say anything to each other, without qualifying or guarding your words, where you share victories and struggles, where there is empathy and conviction, where you spur each other on toward excellence and hold each other accountable not out of duty but out of love. Now, it will not start out that way. It will be awkward at first, starting with baby steps, but if we invest time, and love, and openness, God will give the friendships depth.

Accountability is part of it, but before your eye starts twitching, I am not talking about the accountability that a boss has with an employee, I am talking about having a best friend, a running partner, someone who calls you because he cares about you and sincerely wants to know how you are doing. There is nothing more depressing than going to church week after week, and then missing a few services for whatever reason and no one even noticing that you were missing. No one calls. No one stops by. You could be passed out on your bedroom floor; you could be home with a hundred one fever; you could have fallen into some major sin and be at your most vulnerable point, but no one checks on you. That is not the picture of a church that is devoted to each other, a family, Christ's body. The opposite of love is not hate; it is apathy. If we love each other, if we care about each other's souls, we will hold each other accountable. Every part of the body belongs to all of it, but it is connected to the rest at one point. Our Proverbs 18:24 friendships are the specific bones and tendons that keep us connected. Without them, it is easy, too easy, to drift away.

Proverbs 17:17 states, *" A friend loves at all times, and a brother is born for adversity."*

I know how it is. We have one thousand names in our cell phones. We've been in scores of weddings, served countless people in the church, and are known by everyone. We feel secure that we have countless friends in the kingdom until we face a time of crisis; a family tragedy, an illness, a major spiritual stumble and none of these people are around. Believe me, I've lived this, lived it more than once. Back in 1992 when I contracted a mysterious illness and was bedridden for a year, I was devastated by how few, very few of my friends stood by me. Some of my best buds never called or called once every blue moon. In 2003 when the church I was employed with in Atlanta went through a crisis, it became open season on preachers. It was an extremely challenging time, and once again

I had social leprosy. It happens. It has happened to you; it has happened to me. Like it or not it is part of life.

Human nature says to get bitter and think, "After I've given so much to the kingdom, after I've served So and So and been there for So and So, this is how I get treated. Hmmmmph! At least now I know who my true friends are."   Admit it. We've all felt this way. It is human nature, but it is not the way we need to feel.

First, we need to extend grace. People are flawed; they do not always do right or act right. People can love you, really love you and drop the ball and not be there for you. If you are honest, at some point in your life, you have dropped the ball too. Secondly, you never know what is going on in someone else's life. There may be a good reason why they are not around. Assume the best and extend grace. Lastly, maybe they really are your friends but just not that kind of friend. What do I mean? That Proverbs 17:17 friend is a special friend. There are levels of friendship. There are buds and there are special brothers, brothers born for adversity. Don't resent one for not being the other. Enjoy them for who they are. I'm thankful for my buds, but when the tsunami comes, I need my brothers. My buds love me; they will pray for me, and if I'm on their way, they'll give me a ride out of town. My brother, who was born for adversity, is coming to get me no matter what. If I'm shut in, he'll knock down the wall. If my leg is broken, he'll carry me. If it looks bad, like we won't both make it out, he'll die carrying me, because he cannot bring himself to leave me. He is the brother who was born for adversity. At the end of the day the Proverbs 18:24 friend is the same as the Proverbs 17:17 friend. If I invest in a few friends who are closer than brothers, I'll have a few brothers stand by me during the toughest times. If I do a real good job, I'll have two or three. If I just have a bunch of friends, investing in everyone, getting deep with no one, I'll find that during the time of testing I have companions, but no one to carry my mat and bring me to safety. A man with many companions comes to ruin.

No one gets a crowd during the hardest storms. Jesus who was perfect did not have a crowd stand by him. Of the twelve, only Peter pulled a sword and offered to fight for Him, and only John came back and stood by Him while he died. If you invest in a few spiritual, Proverbs 18:24, friendships, you'll have a few stand by you. If you do not make a conscious effort to invest, you'll have no one. You get out what you put in. You can get bitter, you can get angry at the church, but at the end of the day, unless you have taken the time and made the emotional commitment to build a few special bonds, you have made your own bed? Have you invested? Are you ready for the storm?

God has blessed me with a tremendous number of great friendships over the last twenty-four years and he has blessed me with a handful of special Proverbs 18:24 friendships, more than I deserve. The longest running is my friendship with Mike Patterson, whom I've known since I was twenty-one years old. We were roommates from the time we met until the day I got married, spanning two cities, some interesting living situations, and two many warm memories (This is bonus material: If you are single, get a disciple as a roommate. It's a breeding ground for strong one another friendships). Mike and I have fought; we've laughed; we've pushed each other; we've been there for the good times and the really, really rough times. We've had crossroads where we disagreed and it would have been easier to walk away, but we made the decision to support each other, to love each other even when we haven't seen eye to eye. He has challenged me and called me higher and I like to think I've done the same for him. It's been great, but it has been an investment. The truth is, even with the best friendships, if we do not constantly keep making deposits, there is nothing to withdraw.

Next to my wife, my very best friend is my physical brother Scott, who is both a disciple and an evangelist in New York (technically he is the longest running friendship). Don't laugh;

being best friends with a sibling is no small feat. I am tempted to share about some others, but I'm not. If I start listing them, I'm going to leave somebody out or embarrass someone and have some very angry people on my hands. You know who you are; I love you guys; and I thank God for you.

I will share about one more though. One of my very best friends is Anthony Alford. I had the pleasure of training him when he was first hired as a preacher, after spending eighteen years in the fire department. We became great friends from the time we met, but it was conflict that took it to a new depth. While I was training him, I was pretty heavy handed. Most of the men I had discipled in the ministry were young men. Anthony was a mature man with three sons, one of them grown. He was my friend, I loved him, wanted what was best for him, but I talked down to him and was harsh with him, and made him feel disrespected. I didn't know this. As usual, I thought that I was the most humble, most gracious mentor and friend anyone could ever have. (As I shared earlier, self-deception is my strong suit.) One day, he broke down and shared how much he loved me, but how much I'd hurt him. It was a painful, gut wrenching conversation, but at the end I was so thankful. I was able to apologize and to repent; he had already forgiven me before he had ever approached me. It changed the dynamic of our friendship, adding a component of gut level honesty that is a cornerstone of a Proverbs 18:24 relationship. We became even closer, someone I would die for and would die for me. Being open like that, laying it out there is risky, but the deep bonds are forged through emotional investment and risk taking. If you are afraid to get hurt, you will never again love deeply nor will you be deeply loved.

What are some keys to building Proverbs 18:24 friendships?

Focus on a Few

Pick at least one person, no more than two or three people with whom you will focus on having deep transparent relationship. Be patient; take baby steps; it takes time and you will have a few bumps along the way. Obey the one another scriptures, particularly the ones that take intimacy. You will find that the openness it takes to put these scriptures into practice creates intimacy. Choose someone who has an interest in building a Proverbs 27:17, iron sharpen iron friendship, where you will call each other higher, not enable and make excuses for each other's sins. This person may not be someone with whom you naturally click. Some of my best friendships are with people I never would have hung out with in the world, but Jesus brought us together. Stay with it, persevere with each other, and God will forge something special. If you are serious about this, pick a partner and work hard to make it special.

Invest Time

Chapter II discussed many of the problems found in the Discipling Movement, particularly with the tiered, pyramid style, discipling trees. What was the best part of the old system? In my opinion, the best part is that people were paired up and encouraged (sometimes compelled) to spend consistent time together. Despite all the problems and the weirdness in the way things were done, anytime two disciples consistently spend time together, with an open Bible and a commitment to be open, there is the potential for something good to happen. And often, good things did happen, in spite of us.

I'm not advocating a return to the old structure. What I am saying is that we have to invest time, and the only way to do that is to schedule consistent time together. The older you are, the more responsibilities you have, the more complex life gets, the more we have to fight for time together. If we do not schedule time consistently, religiously, every week, every other week, whatever, it will not happen, and we will be a church of good intentions rather than real one another friendships.

I am all for prayer partners, discipling partners, one another partners, whatever you want to call them as long as it is a true one another partnership. Both sides need to be committed to the relationship and need to schedule consistent time. Married couples desperately need to have at least one couple that can be their Proverbs 27:17, iron sharpens iron couple, where they sharpen each other consistently. About this issue the cliché is definitely true which says, " If you aim at nothing you'll hit it every time." If you do not jealously schedule time, deep one another relationships will remain theory instead of practice.

Be Honest

How is it going for you? Do you have a Proverbs 18:24 friend? I am not asking whether you had one in the past. I am talking about an active relationship. Do you have a Proverbs 27:17 relationship with someone who is sharpening you and you are sharpening? What spiritual man or woman really knows you? Do you aspire to be known? At church, are you lonely in a crowded room, lots of companions but no connection? To whom do you confess your sins, get consistent help with your struggles. Who are you helping?

It is time to get honest, to be real. Remember, if you are not in a Proverbs 18:24 /Proverbs 27:17 relationship you are at risk spiritually. What are you prepared to do? God is calling you to commit to deep spiritual friendships and unlock the door to the one another way.

Healthy Friendships

The key to practically living out the one another way is spiritual friendships, but for these friendships to have their desired effect we need to make sure that they become healthy reciprocal friendships and avoid the traps that Satan will attempt to set. Some of the following areas are particularly susceptible to unhealthy practices.

Advice

Proverbs 15:22 says, *"Plans fail for lack of counsel, but with many advisers they succeed."*

Proverbs 11:14 states, *"For lack of guidance a nation falls but many advisors make victory sure."*

Proverbs 13:10 states, *"Pride only breeds quarrels, but wisdom is found in those who take advice."*

The Bible teaches us to solicit advice before making major decisions and to have the humility to consider and accept wise counsel. In the book of Proverbs and elsewhere in the scriptures, there are countless passages that teach that one of the keys to wisdom is accepting advice and that the way of fools is to not take heed the wisdom of others. Although advice is a valuable tool and along with Bible study and prayer is an essential part of making Godly decisions, when abused it can be a danger rather than an asset. Unscriptural use of advice is a snare that can quickly produce an unhealthy friendship.

What are the keys to the correct use of advice? A few are provided below...

Advice: Key #1

Never seek advice unless you really desire to hear what the person has to say. If your mind is already made up, if you have already firmly decided what you want to do, it is unwise to solicit advice, seeking approval for a decision that has already been made. This will only frustrate the person giving input as well as the person requesting it. A great Biblical example of the folly of this kind of action is found in I Kings 12:1-24. In this passage, the new king Rehoboam, the son of Solomon, solicits advice from Solomon's wise old advisors. He ignores the advice because he had already made up his mind prior to their discussions, so he proceeds to meet with his young friends and have them share what his itching ears wanted to hear. This of course led to disaster.

There is much we can learn from Rehoboam's foolish example. We cannot see ourselves, and we are often too close to the issue to have an objective perspective. We need the wisdom of outsiders before we finalize our decisions. We must be humble enough to know that it is unwise to lean on our own understanding. Having said this, why go through the motions? Do not seek counsel unless you really believe that you need input. God believes that we need advice, but we do not always believe it. Until we see the necessity for advisers, going through the motions is a mutually frustrating exercise.

Advice Key # 2

Advice is just advice. This is huge. As an adult, I do not need another adult's approval, and I do not need anyone's permission. I have the responsibility before God to make the best decision for my family and me. In order to accomplish this, I use the biblical tools for making spiritual decisions. First I pray, I study it out, I seek advice from spiritual men and women with expertise concerning the issue at hand, then I pray some more. I weigh it all, I pray for God's wisdom, but ultimately the decision is mine. If things go wrong, there is no one to blame except me; therefore, I cannot blindly follow someone's advice, no matter whose advice it is, nor can I blame someone else if it does not work out. It is my decision and my responsibility.

Advice Key # 3

Advice is just advice. This is even more important to remember for the person giving the advice. Advice is an opinion. It may be an informed opinion, but in the end it is an opinion and nothing more. It is not scripture. I do not give advice on matters of scripture. I simply open my Bible and share the will of God with someone. God does not give advice. He gives commands. When it is from God, it is not a matter of opinion but a matter of obedience.

God is the only one with this authority. On issues where there is no clear biblical command or principle, we are simply giving advice, meaning we are sharing our best thinking on the topic. No matter how much I may feel that I know best, no matter how much experience I believe I possess on the subject, I do not know for sure. I just think I know.

This is hard. If you love someone, if you really want what is best for him, there is the temptation to be controlling and attempt to make them do what "you know" is best for him. I do not want to see my friends suffer unnecessary hurt and hardship. I do not want to see them make mistakes that I have made or that I have seen countless times. I strongly desire to spare them from that. It is tempting to coerce a friend into making a "wise" decision or to use emotional blackmail and pull away if he does not listen. It is tempting to get angry with a friend who refuses to listen to your "wisdom" and continues making mistakes that you could help him avoid. I have fallen into this temptation and in the name of love become a meddler and an emotional bully rather than a friend. It is unhealthy and it is arrogant, and unfortunately, those of us who struggle with being controlling are the last to see it. We need to listen to and believe others when they point it out.

I still give advice, but the attitude I strive to have on matters of opinion is that I share what I believe is best and why, then I let the matter go. I am supportive of my friends' final decisions whether or not I agree. It is O.K. for friends to disagree, but I need my friends to understand that I respect them and that I love them unconditionally; no strings attached.

It is hard for me to accept, but I am not always right (Why is my wife snickering?). Even on those rare occasions when I do know best, what I have learned the hard way is that adults have to be free to make their own mistakes. <u>God is the ultimate discipler.</u> He will often use our errors to prune and perfect us. We cannot insulate each other from failure. We simply need to be there to help each other up when we fall.

Gossip

There cannot be healthy relationships without trust and there cannot be trust if the person with whom one is sharing his deepest secrets is untrustworthy. Gossip kills relationships.

>   **Proverbs 11:13** *"A gossip betrays a confidence, but a trustworthy man keeps a secret."*

>   **Proverbs 16:28** *"A perverse man stirs up dissension, and a gossip separates close friends."*

>   **Proverbs 18:8** *"The words of a gossip are like choice morsels; they go down to a man's inmost parts."*

No one enjoys being the subject of gossip and one of the great inhibiters to openness is the fear that the person with whom we are sharing might have loose lips. The irony is that as much as we hate someone putting our "business in the streets", we still enjoy gossip when it is about someone else. It really is like choice morsels, one of America's great pastimes, innocent fun, unless the fun is at our expense. The power of this sin is that it draws us in, allowing us to feel justified, to feel like what we are sharing is the exception, that in our case idle chatter is harmless.

But really, if someone shares something personal with me, what right do I have to share it with someone else? When is it not gossip? Surely, if my friend wanted someone else to know, he would share it himself. I can only think of three reasons where it would be appropriate to share something that someone shared with me in confidence.

One reason would be if I had the individual's consent. The second would be if I needed to get advice. For example: If someone were seeking my help with a situation but I needed to seek some advice myself in order to help him, I would do so. But even with this situation, I would make sure that he had full knowledge that I was seeking help (This is important.).

The third reason would be if sharing the information was for the person's own good, be it physical or spiritual. I am not going to keep a secret that hurts people or be a partner to hiding sin. In this case, I would probably confront the individual and challenge him to deal with it, but if he was not willing, I would let him know that I am not going to keep this secret. I would tell him, "If you are not going to come clean and talk to so and so I am". Being a partner to secret sin or a harmful secret is not keeping a confidence. It is being a bad friend. When push comes to shove, I need to fight for my friend's spiritual well being even if he is unwilling to. Yet, even if it is without his consent it is with his knowledge. When I am discussing someone's private life without his knowledge, I am crossing the line.

The truth is, there is a history within discipling ministries of unsafe relationships. There is a history of disciples, especially leaders, justifying gossip under the guise of "discipling" and betraying trust in the name of "shepherding" the flock as if being a leader gives individuals carte blanche to discuss others' lives at will. Once this happens, a dangerous, toxic environment is created that inhibits transparency and gives birth to a culture of fear. If one another relationships are the lifeblood of our churches, then gossip is spiritual AIDS. It is the number one killer.

Do I have the person's consent to share about his life? Am I seeking advice on his behalf and with his knowledge? Am I shedding light on a dangerous secret? If none of these situations apply, why am I discussing details of his life? What right does this other party have to know? Why am I betraying a confidence? Do you want a good litmus test for identifying gossip? Ask yourself how would he feel if the subject of the conversation overheard it? Would he be hurt? Would he be embarrassed? How would he feel if it got back to him what is being discussed? Gossip will destroy our fellowship and undermine trust. It is never innocent and never justified. How can we foster openness and vulnerability if we cannot trust each other? Unless we repent of gossip, we will never have healthy, safe, relationships

Fix Me Friendships

For some disciples, their idea of a one another friendship is that they get with you once a week, they vomit their problems, and you fix them and put them back together. They are extremely eager to spend time. They are quick to initiate to be your "disicpling" partner or to build a great friendship but their definition of a friendship is for you to become a therapist.

In fairness, all of us have times when we are at our lowest point and we need our friends to hear us and help us find strength in the Lord. Over the course of a long friendship, both parties will be in this position on numerous occasions. In a healthy friendship, this may happen on occasion, but it should not define a relationship. To truly be friends, both parties need to go into the relationship with the goal of giving. When the giving is one way, how can a true friendship ever develop? This is draining and laborious for the party seeking to help and develops a weird dependency in those who are constantly seeking to have their emotional needs met. How can this be healthy? Obviously it is not.

It is a symptom of a deeper problem. We need each other, but no relationship can ever fill holes in us that only God himself is meant to fill. We need advice, but advice pales in importance when compared to prayer. We need encouragement, but the ultimate inspiration for us must come from God himself through His word and through his Spirit. The goal of Christian friendships is that we help each other stay focused on God. We must not try to be God for each other. Our friends cannot be the source of our strength; Jesus is. My friends encourage me and point me back to Jesus, but only Jesus can fix me; only He has the answers.

The disciple who gets together with friends in order to get fixed is like an emotional vampire, sucking the life out of others in an effort to get his needs met. He is always dissatisfied. There is always something more his friends can do. Meet more often, call more, help more, listen better, whatever the request, it is never enough. There is a simple reason for this. If Jesus is

<u>not enough, nobody else will be.</u> No friend, no lover, no child, no parent, no one can make a person happy; no one can bring him contentment if he is not finding it in his relationship with God. We need a friend, not a crutch. We need to be partners, not patients. We can point each other to Jesus, but we can never replace Him.

✳ **Career Nurturers**

The other extreme is disciples who feel compelled to mentor and nurture everyone. This type loves to give, serve and meet needs. He is quick to teach, to encourage, or to admonish and willing to serve at a moment's notice. He is always willing to listen when there is sin to be confessed or to give advice and counsel when it is sought and often even when it is not.

Having a friend like this is like having a spiritual mom or dad, a permanent older sibling. In limited doses it can be a good thing and there are times in our lives when we need more than a friend; we need a mentor, but we need mentors for a season, not for life. The challenge with this kind of relationship is that it never changes. Your friend is always willing to help, but never willing to accept it, always willing to help you deal with your sin, but rarely confesses his own and never accepts correction from you when he does. When your friend gives advice, you humbly accept it. When you return the favor, it is met with a condescending nod as if you were a ten year old making a suggestion to a room full of adults. Worse, in some cases you find that your friendship is contingent on you staying dependent. Any attempt to be a peer, to have a reciprocal friendship causes tension. The only way to be content in this "partnership" is to be a permanent child. There is something extremely unhealthy in this type of relationship.

This experience is like being suffocated with love. First it is great, later it is awkward, and eventually it breeds resentment; no one desires to be a career child. I've lived this. Having served in ministries with a hierarchical structure, many of my closest friendships were also often extremely dysfunctional. I have been treated this way and I am sure that I have unknowingly treated others the same. It is ironic, how often we become the very thing that we hate in others, which is one more reason why we should be slow to throw stones. Sometimes mothers and fathers in the faith resist the natural maturing of relationships. Long after both parties have gray hairs, the nurturer still always knows best. Disagreeing is often confused with disloyalty. An attempt to correct and sharpen each other can bring a harsh response or bring on emotional distancing. The worst part of this is that a person who acts this way has no idea this is who he is. He, sincerely, is only attempting to help.

He needs good friends to show him the error of his ways. The challenge is whether he will have the humility to believe them rather than feel attacked or feel that his "spiritual children " have become disloyal. This relationship is unhealthy for both parties and unless the pattern is corrected, both will be hurt.

Conclusion

The goal is not to pass judgment on disciples with these tendencies. We all require a tremendous amount of grace because all of us have made mistakes in relationships. The truth is, in our natural selves, we all lean toward one unhealthy practice or another. The goal is for all of us to honestly evaluate ourselves to see what we need to change in order to be better friends. What is the status of your friendships? What is the cold hard truth of their health? Are you controlling? Are you overly needy? How do others see you? Once we identify our shortcomings, it will take repentance and forgiveness for our friendships to rise to a higher level.

We need friends. We need reciprocal relationships. Friendships that are one sided or hierarchical are unhealthy and in extreme cases can be emotionally dangerous. Let us work hard to build healthy one another relationships and watch God show us the joy of the one another way

David and Jonathan

Romans 15:4 states, *"For everything that was written in the past was written to teach us, so that through endurance and the encouragement of the Scriptures we might have hope."*

In the passage above, the Spirit shares that all of the scriptures from the past, including the Old Testament scriptures, were designed to teach us. Many of the physical challenges experienced by the patriarchs and the kingdom of Israel, are symbolic of the spiritual reality that was to come, the reality now being lived out daily by those who are part of God's eternal kingdom on earth, the Church. Often the history recorded for us in the Old Testament displays graphically spiritual principles that God has established for His church. The friendship of Jonathan and David certainly falls into this category, for it is the perfect example of an intimate, spiritual friendship.

What lessons can we learn from David and Jonathan's friendship?

They Made a Commitment

I Samuel 18:2-4 *"From that day Saul kept David with him and did not let him return to his father's house. And Jonathan made a covenant with David because he loved him as himself. Jonathan took off the robe he was wearing and gave it to David, along with his tunic, and even his sword, his bow and his belt."*

Shortly after David slew Goliath, Jonathan approached David and made a covenant with him. This covenant, which they reaffirmed several times throughout their lifetimes, became the foundation of their partnership. The Hebrew word translated covenant in this passage is the same word used to describe an alliance between nations or a legal bond **[*Definition taken The Hebrew-Greek Key Word Study Bible page 1508]*.** In ancient times, such a covenant was not made lightly and often included the sacrifice of an animal and a public ceremony. It was a serious commitment.

Curiously, the covenant was established before the two personally knew each other. What can we learn from this? We learn that commitment is the basis of a deep spiritual relationship. The friendship and intimacy such a relationship requires is the byproduct of devotion, for devotion is the foundation of family.

Closeness, camaraderie, history, these are the fruits of investment, an investment of time, an investment of trust, and an investment of emotional risk. Until this type of investment is made, true depth in relationships cannot exist. Without devotion our relationships will remain superficial, for the degree of depth is directly proportional to the amount of mutual investment in the relationship.

Many times we want to resist committing until we feel close to someone, withholding any real effort on our part until an emotional connection is established. This is self-defeating because effort is what creates sincere connection. Relationships, be they platonic or romantic, are a gamble, and it is impossible to both guard your heart and give your heart at the same time. In business and in life, investment is a risky business. The key to both is that one must be able to distinguish between a good and a bad investment, in order to avoid disappointment.

Spirituality Was the Foundation of Their Friendship

I Samuel 23:16 *And Saul's son Jonathan went to David at Horesh and helped him find strength in God.*

The key is to invest well. So why did Jonathan choose David? It seems quite obvious what David might gain through being the best friend of the king's son, but how did Jonathan benefit through his devotion to a lowly shepherd?   On the surface, David had everything to gain by their bond and Jonathan absolutely nothing.

From a worldly point of view the two had nothing in common. David was the son of a shepherd while Jonathan was the son of a king. David was from humble means and in all likelihood was relatively uneducated while Jonathan was from royalty and had the finest education in the land. David had the lowest position among the men in his family, being the lastborn son and quite literally the runt of the litter; while, as the firstborn son, Jonathan held the highest position among his siblings. Jonathan was not only a prince; he was the crown prince. They were from different sides of the tracks, had different education levels and were even from different tribes (Jonathan from the tribe of Benjamin and David from Judah). What could possibly be the basis of Jonathan's choice?

I Samuel 18:1 *"After David had finished talking with Saul, Jonathan became one in spirit with David and he loved him as himself."*

David had just slain Goliath and led Israel to a rousing victory. Afterwards, Saul summoned David to him and spoke with him. After witnessing David's conversation with his father the scriptures tell us that Jonathan became one with David in spirit. Why? I believe that Jonathan recognized two special qualities in him, courageous faith and selflessness.

Jonathan too was a man of faith who had trusted God and seen victories in battles against overwhelming odds. In I Samuel chapter fourteen, Jonathan on his own, accompanied only by his armor bearer, attacked the Philistine army, armed with the confidence that God was with him. With unwavering faith that the Lord had delivered the Philistine army into his hands, Jonathan threw himself into battle against all logic. He saw his faith rewarded and he led Israel to an improbable victory that day. People of faith are rare. People who do great works out of selflessness rather than for their own glory are more so. In David, Jonathan saw a kindred spirit, someone who loved God as he did, someone willing to put his faith into action and to risk everything to uphold the name of the Lord Almighty. Seeing David's heart for God, there was nothing else that Jonathan needed to know. David was the man to whom he would pledge his life; he would be the friend who is closer than a brother.

Jonathan invested well. He did not look for someone from the same background, the same race, same age, or the same class. He did not put the emphasis on personality or common interests. Jonathan invested in spirituality. It is important to have friendships with depth, but deep friendships with unspiritual people will not save you in the time of trouble. In Luke chapter five, a paralytic is brought to Jesus carried on a mat by his friends. When they could not get inside the house where Jesus was because of the crowd, they climbed up on the roof, made a hole and lowered the man down (I'm sure the owner loved that).

Luke 5:20 *"When Jesus saw their faith, he said, 'Friend, your sins are forgiven.'"*

Jesus was impressed by the faith of the paralytic's friends and the paralytic's life was blessed because of it. The paralytic invested well. The question for us is simple: What do our closest friendships say about us? Is Jesus impressed by the faith of your friends? Are you drawn to men and women with a radical passion for God or do you avoid them? Are you only drawn to people like yourself? The basis of Jonathan's friendship with David was spirituality, and this common denominator was greater than all of their differences. If we are to have Proverbs 18:24 friendships, we need to imitate the example of these men. We will forge life-changing partnerships that cross every cultural, racial, and economic line with our love for Jesus being the common foundation.

This should go without saying, but if this principle applies to platonic friendships, it is even more essential for romantic relationships. Giving away your heart is an investment. Are you most attracted to the physical or the spiritual? Is finding a "successful" mate your prime objective or is seeking a mate with Godly character your primary qualification? Is Jesus impressed by the faith of your love interests?   In love and in friendship the basis of our most intimate relationships must be a sincere love for God.

In February of 2006, I started a course on real estate investment and in addition to classroom lessons, the course involved mentorship from an experienced investor. The key to becoming a successful investor is recognizing the difference between a good and bad deal. The numbers must add up, and for the particular investment model I was learning, the repairs needed to be $25,000 or less (with few exceptions). Initially it was confusing. Crunching the numbers was easy for me, but learning to see property from an investor's perspective was not. Initially, I was too hard on property seeing it through the eyes of a homeowner rather than a businessman. Under this model we bought, repaired, rented and re-sold "ugly homes". I'd walk into a home and my mentor would ask me what I thought. I'd say, "This home is horrible, not worth the time. My guess is that it will take $50,000 or more to fix it up." My mentor would smile and say, "This home is perfect. We can fix it up with about $20,000 and make $40,000 profit when we're done," and then he would proceed to explain why.

After a few weeks of this, I thought I was ready. I went out and made offers on several houses and was excited when one of my bids was accepted. The house needed a large amount of work, more than usual, but it had an incredible amount of equity and my offer was accepted with a bid much less than what the owner was asking, further increasing the potential for profit. I was excited and brought my mentor down to see it. When he saw it, he shook his head and told me that the house was worthless. I was stunned. Sure it needed more work than normal, but the numbers were impressive. There was an amazing amount of equity in the property. My mentor pointed to the foundation. I had become so caught up in the numbers and the potential that I failed to notice that the foundation was completely rotted. Without a foundation, I was not buying a house. All I was buying was a few blades of grass. Fortunately for me, he was able to get me out of the deal but I learned an important lesson that day. When investing you can take a gamble on a lot of things, but you cannot invest in a bad foundation. I needed to start with the foundation and work my way up from there.

Relationships are exactly the same way. Any life not built on Jesus (Luke 6:46-49) is built on a bad foundation. Neither Islam, nor Buddha, nor self-help books, nor anything else can be a substitute for Jesus, and watered down Christianity is an equally treacherous foundation. The solid rock that we build our lives upon must be the truth, so any friendship not based on the Lord will never provide shelter through the storms. Jonathan understood that a spiritual foundation is the key to investing well. We would do well to imitate his wisdom.

Their Friendship was Intimate

I Samuel 20:41 *After the boy had gone, David got up from the south side of the stone and bowed down before Jonathan three times, with his face to the ground. Then they kissed each other and wept together—but David wept the most.*

I Samuel 20:17 *And Jonathan had David reaffirm his oath out of love for him, because he loved him as he loved himself.*

II Samuel 1:25-26   *"How the mighty have fallen in battle! Jonathan lies slain on your heights. I grieve for you, Jonathan my brother; you were very dear to me. Your love for me was wonderful, more wonderful than that of women."*

What has always struck me about the relationship between Jonathan & David was the intimacy of their relationship and as a man it is humbling that two men could be so vulnerable and open with each other, so free to express their emotions. Sinful minds have often tried to warp this passage and use this to justify homosexuality, reasoning that the only way that two men could be so close would be if they were sexually involved. This is a ridiculous assertion. Homosexuality is strongly and consistently condemned throughout the scriptures (Romans 1:24-27), and Jonathan and David were righteous men, committed to living Godly lives. Such corrupted thinking misses the power of these passages. These verses underscore our incredible need for close, same gender friendships, for there are some things that we need from sister to sister, brother to brother camaraderie that we cannot possibly attain from the opposite gender.

As a man, I know that, at their best, my male friendships push me in ways that my wife never can and understand me in ways that she never will. When I have pushed through my natural superficiality and the pride and competitiveness that are often the bane of brotherhood, I have found incredible life changing relationships. The brothers fill a need spiritually and emotionally that cannot be met any other way, and I know my wife feels the same about her closest sisters in Christ. The trick is opening up, humbling out, and creating true trust and transparency. If we are willing to risk much, God will reward us with bonds forged by the blood of Christ, which are intimate and unbreakable.

Their Friendship Was Devoid of Hierarchy

I Samuel 18:4 *"Jonathan took off the robe he was wearing and gave it to David, along with his tunic and even his sword, his bow and his belt."*

In ancient times, it was common for warriors to exchange weapons and even armor as a sign of respect [**Adam Clarke's Commentary**]. Still, Jonathan placing his robe on David had even greater significance because Jonathan's robe was a symbol of his royalty. While scholars debate the exact purpose of this gesture, it is my conviction that the reason for it is fairly simple.

By placing the robe on David, Jonathan was elevating him to his status, showing through a simple gesture that their friendship would be a friendship of equals. There would be no status or hierarchy between them. Theirs was not a relationship of prince and subject. From that day forth they would be brothers.

Titles, and status can be tremendous stumbling blocks to the type of bonds that God intends to forge among His people. In congregations, leadership and structure can often produce unintended and unnecessary barriers. Spiritual leadership is of God, and no organization can be effective without some structure, but structure exists to serve us not for us to serve structure. God ordained that congregations have elders, evangelists, and teachers to lead His church (Ephesians 4:11) and deacons to perform roles of service (I Timothy 3:8-13). In addition, in an effort to imitate the ministry of Jesus, congregations often appoint small group leaders to help shepherd and disciple God's people. In their proper place, these positions work to strengthen the church, but when our sinful nature gets in the way, they greatly impede the work of the Holy Spirit.

Our first relationship with each other as disciples of Christ is as brothers and sisters. This fact supersedes any title ever held or responsibility ever given. We are brothers first, on equal ground before the foot of the cross. Yet, too often an ungodly hierarchy develops among relationships, and unfortunately, the worst offenders of this practice are church leaders themselves.

In twenty-two years as a minister of the gospel, I have witnessed a scarcity of healthy peer relationships among church leaders. More often than not, the leaders with the most authority give instruction, guidance, and correction, and the rest simply accept it. Correction, instruction, and guidance do not develop both ways. Often, it seems as if the church is imitating the corporate model of the world, with the elders or lead evangelist as CEO's rather than imitating the pattern of family we see in scripture. Until the leaders of congregations forge Proverbs 18:24 relationships unencumbered by title, the church will remain relationally dysfunctional. Yes, the evangelist must be humble enough to accept shepherding, teaching, and correction from the elders, but the elders in kind must accept correction training, and guidance from the evangelist. Leaders have different gifts and the nature of leadership in a church family is gift based rather than title based. Until the leadership functions as wings on a plane, as peers and brothers with iron sharpening iron friendships, the church will never truly soar. The church leadership must form a brotherhood where all parties can speak openly and honestly with no fear of repercussion and where there is humility among all parties, enabling them to learn from one another.   Too often an environment is created where honesty is not rewarded and the "lesser" leader finds that he must watch his words or jeopardize his standing as a leader. Such an environment may breed success in corporate or military settings, but in a church it is crippling. It is time that leaders put aside their robes and learn to build family.

I've seen titles perform a weird transformation on even the best-hearted disciples. I have witnessed congregations destroyed because great brothers with little experience in church leadership became elders and suddenly acted as if they had become experts in every facet of church affairs, overriding the counsel of evangelists with over thirty years of experience in church building. I have seen evangelists arrogantly lead, ignoring the wise counsel, of elders, other evangelists, and mature brothers in their ministries and have their lives and their ministries devastated as a result of their pride. In my time in the ministry, I have witnessed this dysfunction first hand and sadly, at various times, my own sin has contributed to it.

It is not just evangelist and elders who are guilty. We have all witnessed that kind hearted brother in the back of the church appointed the head usher and become instantly transformed into a fire breathing drill sergeant; yet, the key to the problem and the solution begins with those charged with directing the affairs of the church. Elders and evangelist must grow beyond the endless and ridiculous debate over who gets the final say in church matters and like Jonathan take the step of exchanging robes. For a church to truly be Christ's church it must be family, and the success or failure of any family begins at the top. Until, elders, evangelists, and teachers forge relationships with depth based on the principles of Proverbs 18:24, Proverbs 27:17, and Proverbs 17:17, there is little hope for the long- term success of the congregations they lead. They must become so much more than merely co-workers and their brotherhood must not merely be for show. Too often, I have observed "men of God" proclaim their undying love and friendship for each other in public when privately they fought like Ali and Frazier, all smiles and hugs for the masses but inwardly they harbored resentment and dissension that they had carried for years. How can we expect God to bless a church whose leadership is engaged in such duplicity? For the church to be family, its leaders must become men who are closer than brothers; they must form iron sharpen iron relationships where they are free to challenge and perfect one another, and they must become the brothers who were born for adversity, loyally standing by each other not turning on one another when the storms come. Unless these three proverbs describe the relational dynamic of your church leadership group, your church is at risk. God's church is fueled by faith, hope, and love and those He has appointed to lead must exemplify that love. Like Jonathan, it is time that church leaders took off their robes and gave it to their brother.

Conclusion

In Jonathan and David, we see a tremendous template of true spiritual brotherhood. If we dare to imitate their example, we will tear down the superficial barriers that divide us and learn to build powerful life long friendships built on the solid foundation of Jesus. Who is your Jonathan? Who is your David? Have you invested well? Have you invested at all? These questions are among the most important of our spiritual lives. It is time that we give our hearts, exchange our robes, and find that friend who is closer than a brother.

Honesty

If you search for tenderness
It isn't hard to find
You can have the love you need to live
But if you look for truthfulness
You might just as well be blind
It always seems to be so hard to give

Honesty is such a lonely word
Everyone is so untrue
Honesty is hardly ever heard
And mostly what I need from you

-Billy Joel (from the song "Honesty")

Billy Joel may not be a prophet, but his lyrics for the song, "Honesty" resonate with scriptural truth. Honesty is rare. In the world, it is virtually extinct; but even, in the church, truthfulness is an endangered species. Because we are people pleasers, because we are conflict avoiders, because too often, we are politicians instead of prophets, and because we refuse to believe that it is the truth not human wisdom that sets us free, we frequently, shade the truth, color the truth, spin the truth, distort it in the name of shrewdness, and selectively distribute it, believing Satan's lie that we are somehow protecting each other when we are in fact undermining the foundation of our relationships. God is not wrong. A partial truth is a total lie and His way, the path of honesty and total transparency, is always best, with no exceptions. Honesty and biblical conflict resolution are cornerstones to effectively restoring the one another way in our fellowships.

Proverbs 27:5-6 *"Better is open rebuke than hidden love. Wounds from a friend can be trusted, but an enemy multiplies kisses."*

Proverbs 28:23 *"He who rebukes a man will in the end gain more favor than he who has a flattering tongue."*

Ephesians 4:14-16 *"Then we will no longer be infants, tossed back and forth by the waves, and blown here and there by every wind of teaching and by the cunning and craftiness of men in their deceitful scheming. Instead, speaking the truth in love, we will in all things grow up into him who is the Head, that is, Christ."*

The scriptures make it clear that disciples must be honest in every situation, being honest with each other even when the truth hurts. Proverbs 27:5-6 teaches us that a true friend will share difficult truths while an enemy will tell us only what we desire to hear. In Proverbs 28:23 the Spirit reveals that in the end the person who shares the difficult truths will be better received than the one who avoids conflict. Through Ephesians 4:15 we learn that the motivation for being truthful with each other must be love. We must be loving in the way that we communicate and we must let love be our only agenda. When we hold back, concerned about a friend's response, we are in fact more committed to ourselves, avoiding any negative repercussions that we might face, than truly concerned about the spiritual well being of our friend. We have to love our friends enough to put our friendships on the line. We need to love their souls enough to fight for their relationships with God even if it puts our friendships at risk. Why? Because the truth is what is best even when it does not feel like it could possibly be. Because God's way is right even when we cannot understand how it will all work out. God is light; He is honest; He is real. In His path there are no shades of gray. "What if the truth is painful?" we ask. "What someone doesn't know can't hurt them," is the wisdom of our time. Yet God's response is found in scripture.

Isaiah 55:8-10 *"For my thoughts are not your thoughts, neither* *are your ways my ways,' declares the Lord 'As the heavens are higher than the earth, so are my ways higher than your ways and my thoughts than your thoughts."*

His ways are not our ways, but if we are to walk in the light, we must learn the ways of our master. Because it is impossible for God to lie (Hebrews 6:18), so it must be with us. Transparency runs contrary to worldly logic and sometimes contrary to even our own instincts for survival. Complete honesty will lead to more conflict; it will lead to accepting accountability for our mistakes rather than covering them up; it will lead to openness and vulnerability in our relationships, stripping us of all facades; it will unveil hidden agendas and covert manipulation; it will lead to more apologies; it will require more humility and mountains and mountains of grace because we have much to confess and much to forgive. Complete truthfulness will complicate things and is sure to lead us out of our comfort zones, but it will lead to something else as well. It will set us free (John 8:32).

There is a freedom in being known and truly knowing others. There is a freedom in having a few close comrades with whom we can bare all and be gut level real, knowing that they accept us and love us as we are, with no facades. A tremendous burden is lifted when we have partners with whom we can confess our sins who will not judge us or look down on us, but will love us enough to tell us what we need to hear, and be there to help us to make changes so that we can glorify God. Satan can no longer accuse us because we have nothing to hide. Too often we are so guarded in our communication, so careful. I need to have my Proverbs 18:24 brothers and sisters with whom I can vent and cut loose, knowing they will always assume the best and help me get back on course. I know I cannot see myself clearly, that I am the last one to see my own sin. It gives me a sense of security to know that I have people in my life who know me and will love me enough to tell me the truth, even when it hurts.

The truth will set us free. Most of us are only honest with our friends and even our spouses up to a point, keeping our guards up so that we will not get hurt, afraid to be fully exposed and have our weakness and frailty become evident to all. We want intimacy but we fear it. We crave honesty, but it terrifies us. Yet, until we get gut level honest, our interaction will always be superficial. The older I get the less I am attracted to superficial friendships. For me, personally, I believe the number one quality I need in friendship is complete honesty and transparency. The older I get, the less patience I have for those who have mastered the art of almost saying something, or those who always share the "truth" with a spin. Vulnerability may be risky business, but its absence is empty and unsatisfying. I prefer the complications that come with truthfulness to the relative safety of plastic interaction. If we are going to have dynamic one another relationships we are going to need to learn to reach a new level of honesty and to biblically resolve the conflict that comes from honest communication.

Crave Honesty

The first step to building honest relationships is that we have to desire them, desire them in our inmost beings. We have to invite our friends to be real with us, making it easy for them to speak with us about even the most sensitive issues and communicating approachability in both our verbal and nonverbal communication. I have a picture of myself, a picture that is distorted by my own pride and ego. In my eyes, I am smarter than I really am, I am better looking, I am funnier, I am super humble, and I am almost always right. Even when I look in the mirror, I fool myself into thinking I am skinnier than I am. I'm always shocked when I see a photograph at how different I look in the picture than how I think I look and in my most delusional moments, I will blame the difference on a bad camera angle rather than on all those bags of corn chips over the last six months. My pride is a drug and I am an addict constantly living under the influence, making me blind to myself and sometimes just out right stupid. Even when I think I'm sober, I am probably functioning with a buzz, a victim of a powerful delusion. I only have two things working in my favor:

the word of God and good friends

The word of God is living and active, sharper than any blade, stripping away all illusions and pretense (Hebrews 4:12-13). The Bible is a mirror that reveals our true selves and empowers us to transform from who we are into the image of God (James 1:23-25). The scriptures are our first and most formidable tool to assist us in gaining self knowledge. Trusting our opinions, our feelings, our education, human expertise, the insight of others, traditions, or even our upbringing over the word of God is sheer folly and will surely lead us down an endless cycle of self-deception. Our feelings are a particularly shaky foundation on which to place our trust because when we feel something strongly it feels true even if it is not. Who I really am is not who I feel I am but who the scriptures say I am.

> **Jeremiah 17:9** *"The heart is deceitful above all things and beyond cure. Who can understand it?"*

> **Proverbs 28:26** *"He who trusts in himself is a fool, but he who walks in wisdom is kept safe."*

We must be students of the word, opening wide our hearts to both its insights about the Father and about us, letting the Bible be our standard, a shining star guiding us out of the maze of darkness and misdirection that Satan has erected to lead us astray. Yet, although the word is our primary guide, sometimes even when reading it, we cannot make the connection for ourselves. For this reason, the Spirit sends people to us to illuminate the areas that remain hidden.

If you have a spiritual friend who loves you and will always speak the truth to you even when it hurts, you have a rare treasure, a gift from God. I covet and protect these types of relationships because I have come to realize how very precious they are and how difficult they are to find. We all have far too many sycophants in our lives that will tell us exactly what we want to hear. This is how the discussion tends to go.

You say, "Joe said I was wrong. Can you believe it? What do you think Ralph?"

"No, man you're cool," he says, knowing full well you are dead wrong.

You say, "Man, Janet says that this tie and shirt make me look like an old man. Can you believe it? What do you think Ralph?"

"No, man, you're cool," he says, knowing he would never, ever, ever wear that tie in a million years.

If people had honest friends, American Idol would go out of

business. We've all seen the try out segments, when all of these tone deaf people audition and we have watched their shock when Simon Cowell tells them that they are pitiful. Are we to seriously believe that none of their family, or friends, or even their voice teachers (many of them say that they have been taking voice lessons) have ever noticed that their buddy couldn't sing a lick? As a former choir director, I can tell you that it is not just TV. You would be surprised at the number of people who have auditioned for our choir over the years believing and having been told their whole lives that they sounded like Mariah Carey when in fact they were quite vocally challenged. I would tell them as nicely as I could that being a soloist is definitely not their calling, only to have many of them get angry with me. Now really, was I the first person to notice that they could not sing or simply the first one to be honest with them? As the saying goes, "Friends don't let friends drive drunk."

Judgment day will be like American idol. People that have had no one tell them the truth during their lifetimes will be, exposed, shocked to learn how God really sees them. We need to surround ourselves with people who will tell us what we need to hear rather than those who share what we want to hear and we need to listen when they speak. Yes, what they are saying is different than the crowd, but truth is rarely found in following the herd. Crave honesty, search it out, and treat it as a precious jewel. These friendships are among your most valuable possessions.

Pay the Price for Honesty

There is a reason why so many people are reluctant to be
honest. Honesty comes at a price. I would like to be able to say
that if we are truthful with our friends, it will always be
appreciated, but that simply is not the case. Sometimes, our
friends will be thankful, sometimes, it will lead to conflict and
after the conflict is resolved, they will appreciate the straight
forwardness and the relationship will be closer for it, and
sometimes, we will lose our friends over the truth. Honesty is a
risky business. The truth hurts and sometimes it is the
messenger who experiences the most piercing pain.

Matthew 5:10 *"Blessed are those who are persecuted because of
righteousness, for theirs is the kingdom of heaven."*

If we are righteous, if we are truthful, it will lead to conflict and
even persecution. Now, I am not referring to the type of trouble
we bring on ourselves by being harsh or obnoxious. Some
people, who pride themselves on their forthrightness, confuse a
lack of tact and timing with frankness. A lack of people skills is
not among the fruits of the spirit, and bluntness unaccompanied
by empathy, grace and compassion, deservedly, will never be
well received. We are to speak the truth in love, imitating the

heart and spirit of Jesus. Yet, Jesus, who was perfect, expressed himself lovingly and flawlessly and was still murdered by religious people for speaking the truth. If we are to be His disciples, we must walk as Jesus did.

Recently, I was listening to an evangelist, Will Archer, preach an amazing sermon and one of his points was that we must pay the price for truth. His point was that we must love each other enough to be forthright even if we know there will be negative repercussions. It was a great point, and for me, personally, it was extremely convicting. The goal is to help each other make it to heaven, and if we see something that can inhibit our brother from making it, we must love him enough to point it out, in love, regardless of the cost. When your brother repents, short time or long, he will love you for your help. If he never repents, your conscience will be clear. If you ignore his sin, fearing the worst, how sincere is your love? True love is selfless, making one willing to sacrifice himself for the good of his brothers. Truth is always what is good.

This is not the way of the world, but we do not belong to the world. We are Christ's church; our citizenship is in heaven. This is not our world; this is not our nation. We have our own country, our own culture, and our own language. In God's kingdom, heaven is our nation, the blood of Christ is our race, faith is our passport, love is our language, and truth is our culture. We must be the one place in the world where there is real unity and where truth is rewarded; yet, too often to our shame this is not the case. Too often the church is contaminated by the world, adopting its culture and adapting to its ways. Too often people pleasing, gossip, and manipulation threaten to strangle the life out of our relationships. Sadly, even in the church, flattery and superficiality are often rewarded and honesty is punished.

How can we transform this culture into the culture of truth? We need brothers and sisters who have the courage to be honest, in love, to speak up. Too often we are waiting for the spiritual climate to change before we will speak up, but taking a stand is what creates change. There are too many pink elephants in our congregations. If we fail to speak an obvious truth, we become partners to an obvious lie. We must speak the truth in love.

It is important to remember that we must speak truth in love and never in anger. Once anger and frustration enter the equation, it is easy for Satan to take hold, corrupting the message into venom that will threaten the foundation of our fellowships. As disciples, how we say things is as important as what is being said. If it is not said in love, what we are saying may be right, but we have ceased to be righteous. Without righteousness our words are worthless, bankrupt of the Spirit's power.

In the church as a whole and in our closest relationships, truth must be our culture. Honesty will test friendships, but friendships need to be tested. If the foundation is sound, forthrightness will serve to deepen the bond. If the truth spoken lovingly can permanently damage a partnership, it was built on a shaky foundation. The light of truth will reveal the health of our relationships. Sometimes it is scary, but if we pay the price for honesty, we will also reap its incredible blessings.

Biblically Resolve Conflict

Matthew 6:14-15 *"For if you forgive men when they sin against you, your heavenly Father will also forgive you. But if you do not forgive men their sins, your Father will not forgive your sins."*

Matthew 18:15-17 *"If your brother sins against you, go and show him his fault, just between the two of you. If he listens to you, you have won your brother over. But if he will not listen, take one or two others along, so that 'every matter may be established by the testimony of two or three witnesses. If he refuses to listen to them, tell it to the church; and if he refuses to listen even to the church, treat him as you would a pagan or a tax collector."*

Matthew 5:23-24 *"Therefore, if you are offering your gift at the altar and there remember that your brother has something against* *you, leave your gift there in front of the altar. First go and be reconciled to your brother; then come and offer your gift"*

Honesty leads to conflict, not necessarily because it creates more conflict, but because truthful dialogue will bring to the surface feelings and attitudes that we would otherwise suppress. When plastic smiles and half-hearted hugs are replaced with straightforward discussion, sparks are going to fly. When true feelings are unspoken, they fester like a cancer beneath the surface, with no hope of a cure. Honesty leads to conflict, but because we are in Christ, disagreements can be resolved and the process of discussing and resolving issues adds depth and closeness to our friendships. The key is that we must follow God's plan for conflict resolution. There are five keys to biblical resolution: Prayer, Bible study, unconditional grace, an urgent desire to reconcile, and a willingness to go the extra mile.

There is no hope of reconciliation until there is forgiveness, and forgiveness must be sincere and unconditional. We are commanded to forgive one another (Matthew 6:14-15) with no strings attached. It does not matter if the other party sees his wrong or if he ever repents. We still have the responsibility to forgive. God has the right to put conditions on our forgiveness, but we, who are all sinners, do not have the right to place conditions on one another. Too many disciples enter conversations reserving their grace toward each other until they see what the other person's response will be. Grace is free. Once we have extended grace freely and unconditionally, forgiving not because the other person is deserving but because Christ has forgiven us, then we are ready to proceed toward reconciliation. Reconciliation is not a given. Both parties need to desire it for it to be achieved, but grace can be given unilaterally. Whether my brother ever forgives me has no bearing on me forgiving him. I give grace because grace is what God has given me. I do not have the right to hold a grudge.

We need to urgently desire to reconcile, understanding the goal is to reconcile, not to be vindicated. The objective must be to bridge the gap and heal the wounds, not to prove that we are right and the other person is wrong. As long as we are trying to prove our point, the rift will only increase. It is possible to disagree on matters of opinion and still be completely united. Reconciliation is about restoring unity not about pleading our case. Matthew 5:23-24 makes it clear that the Lord expects us to have a sense of urgency about unity, being willing to drop everything in order to be reconciled with our brothers and having the humility to be the initiator of peace, even if we feel we are the one who was wronged. In God's eyes, there is nothing more important than fighting for our relationships.

We must be willing to go the extra mile for unity, following the Biblical steps for establishing it. In the world we generally handle conflict in one of three ways: We blow up at the person who hurt us, we stuff it, saying "it's no big deal," and let it eat us up inside, or we talk to our other friends, gossiping about it, but do not speak to the person who offended us. All three worldly practices are doomed to failure. In Matthew 18:15-17, God lays out His process, a process that works. Specifically, the passage addresses how to speak with someone who has sinned against us, but the principle extends to all conflict, even doing wonders for marital disputes.

The scripture directs us to go to our brother and show him his fault, just between us two. If that does not go well, we are to involve two or three other disciples and discuss the matter altogether. In matters of sin, if the issue is still unresolved, we are to bring it before the church. Why go to the brother first? It prevents gossip, or different disciples choosing sides as they hear only one side of the story. A one on one conversation prevents misunderstanding and hopefully will lead to openness and bonding. If both sides desire reconciliation, it is amazing what the Spirit can accomplish in a simple heart to heart discussion. If that does not go well, the two should agree on some spiritual brothers who can help mediate the discussion. It is important for both parties to be there with the group so that the brothers can hear both sides. With prayer and scripture most matters can be settled at this point.

God's plan for reconciliation works, but the problem in too many cases is that disciples do not give God's plan a chance. We quit on each other, avoiding each other rather than urgently meeting in order to become re-united, we make the issue being right rather than being reconciled, and we stubbornly refuse to forgive. Often, disciples, simply refuse to put Matthew 18:15-17 into practice, the simple command to go to your brother first, just between the two of you. This passage is one of the least obeyed scriptures in God's word, and church leaders are often the worst offenders, devising complex rationalizations and dubious theology to justify an unwillingness to simply obey and to call their members to do the same. I have had more than one prominent leader tell me, " I know him. He won't listen any way," as their justification for not going to their brother and attempting to work it out, sharing their hurt with their spouses and other friends but never directly with the party who offended them. Other leaders, cowardly, will ambush each other in small groups with matters that they should have discussed privately first. God is not wrong. We will never disobey His commands without consequence and all of our reasons why our situation is the "exception" will not change that fact. Until we have the humility to submit to the Lord's wisdom on this issue, relationships in the church will remain dysfunctional. I have seen numerous church splits in the last several years. Many have at their root unresolved personal conflict between church leaders. There is a better way, God's way. Will we listen?

It takes one to forgive, but two to reconcile. The question for us individually is have we done everything in our power to reconcile with our brothers? Have we forgiven, initiated peace, humbled ourselves, gone to them privately, and sought mediation. Have we assumed how our brother or sister will respond or have we given them the benefit of the doubt and given the Holy Spirit a chance. God has power to heal. If we will follow His plan, He will lead us to resolution and to deeper, healthier relationships, built on truth.

The One Another Way

We've spent the last several chapters discussing in detail keys to implementing the one another way, specifically as it pertains to developing special friends who are closer than brothers. If we put these principles into practice, they will serve us well and will help us to build these valuable relationships. With that being said, it is important to understand that if we put the one another scriptures into practice we will develop many different types of friendships, each meeting different needs.

We need to find our Jonathans and Davids but a healthy Christian walk will develop a large number of relationships with various levels of closeness, reflecting different sides of our personalities. We will have fathers and mothers of the faith, little brothers and sisters, hang out buddies, etc. We need to appreciate each one for what it is rather than be critical of what it is not. In Christ, I have had the privilege to love and be loved by a large army of brothers and sisters. Each relationship is special in its way and all are important.

I need to enjoy them all but not lose focus on the fact that I still need to invest in a few in order to develop friendships at the deepest level. I get to taste the one another way in all my friendships but it is with my Proverbs 18:24 friends that I feel the full extent of its power. If we do not invest in forging these bonds, we will never truly know the full glory of the one another way.

The Truth About Discipling

Definition of Discipling:

The Greek word translated to disciple is Matheteuo. A more complete definition of Matheteuo is: "To be or to make to be a disciple, to disciple to make a disciple to train as a follower, instruct as an adherent, mentor. The action of the verb describes much more than academic impartation of information, it suggests the shaping of character and the cultivation of a world-view through a close, personal relationship between student and teacher" [**Definition taken from The Hebrew-Greek Key Word Study Bible page 1647**].

As significant as one another relationships are, discipling is equally important. If the one another commands constitute the heart of the church then discipling can best be described as its nervous system. All the directives from the head, Jesus, are best communicated with the aid of discipling. If it breaks down, the whole body malfunctions. Without effective discipling, a congregation can still see an increase of members, but it will never see a multiplication of committed disciples unless there is a commitment to the type of personal teaching and training that defined Jesus' ministry. Jesus laid the foundation for the church and spent three years teaching his followers how to properly and effectively build upon it, equipping them with both the message and the method. Discipling is Jesus' method of choice. If we have any hope of building, dynamic, healthy ministries, it must become ours as well.

Jesus' Way

What was Jesus' way? His objective was simple: to save the world. The first part of the plan is found in His death and resurrection, becoming a sacrifice through whom all men have the opportunity to be redeemed. The second part involved laying the foundation for His church, the kingdom of God on earth. So how did He go about the business of church building? Did he focus on the masses? Did He set up a university, dedicated to equipping church leaders? No, His plan was not so grandiose. He focused on a few.

Mark 3:13-15 *"Jesus went up on a mountainside and called to him those he wanted, and they came to him. He appointed twelve designating them apostles that they might be with him and that he* *might send them out to preach and to have authority to drive out demons."*

Matthew 9:36-10:1 *"When he saw the crowds, he had compassion on them, because they were harassed and helpless, like sheep without a shepherd. Then he said to his disciples, "The harvest is plentiful but the workers are few. Ask the Lord of the harvest, therefore, to send out workers into his harvest field. He called his twelve disciples to him and gave them authority to drive out evil spirits and to heal every disease and sickness."*

Jesus appointed twelve men and designated them apostles with the goal of walking with them and sending these men out to preach and perform miracles. These twelve were the cornerstones of His movement. He invested in the apostles and through them His work would be completed after His ascension and the good news of the gospel would be spread throughout the world. Jesus' ministry lasted only about three years. Knowing His time was short, His work was fueled by an incredible sense of urgency. He focused on what He knew would be most effective. While he did not ignore the masses, they were not His chief concern. The majority of His time was spent walking with and training a few, in order to raise up leaders and workers for the task of world evangelism.

He focused on small groups of leaders spending most of His time with three, the three who would be the pillars of the early church, Peter, James, and John. In the garden of Gethsamene (Matthew 26:36-39), at Jairus' house (Luke 8:51-56), at the transfiguration (Luke 9:28-36), and elsewhere, we see Jesus spending special time with these three, apart from the rest of the twelve. In addition to the three, Jesus invested an enormous amount of time with the twelve, mentoring them, molding their character, shaping their faith, teaching them how to pray, even helping one walk on water. In every way, He discipled them. While Most of His ministry was dedicated to equipping the three and the twelve, in addition to these groups, Jesus instructed and sent out the seventy-two (Luke 10:1-4). Jesus spent time with the crowds, the seventy-two, the twelve, and the three. The smaller the group, the greater His investment of time, giving the least to the greatest numbers of people and the most to the fewest. On the surface, this may seem counter-productive, but this was His way. He concentrated His efforts on the three and the twelve, and at the end of His life had very little besides them to show for His efforts.

By superficial standards, Jesus' ministry was a failure. He spent three years building a ministry, preaching and teaching throughout Judea. In addition to His oratory skills, Jesus had the added advantage of confirming His message with signs wonders and miracles, a great way to draw a crowd if ever there was one. His parting act was the greatest miracle of all, for after His resurrection, He came and visited the surviving eleven apostles, His brother James, and over five hundred other disciples (I Cor. 15:3-8). Yet, for all this, shortly after Christ's ascension, only one hundred twenty were numbered among the believers (Acts 1:15). Where were the other four hundred people who saw the resurrected Lord? Where were all the crowds who saw His miracles? Where were all the thousands who professed to be His disciples during Jesus' lifetime? After everything, His ministry was reduced to one hundred twenty disciples. In all probability, it consisted of the eleven surviving apostles, Mary, Jesus' mother, and the women who had supported him (Acts1:14), Jesus' physical brothers (Acts 1:14), probably the seventy-two and not much else. By the numbers, there is nothing impressive about what Jesus built. I have known preachers to build churches of thousands in a few years time. If we are determining success purely by members in pews, Jesus failed.

But numbers were not Jesus' concern. His ministry was not about converting the masses but molding leaders who in turn would preach to the world. In the upper room were one hundred twenty leaders, men and women who had been discipled by Jesus to maturity. In addition, the eleven apostles had been molded to be leaders of leaders, who would continue to direct the ministry after Christ's return to glory. Shortly after their gathering in the upper room, Jesus' followers witnessed an incredible miracle, the conversion of three thousand souls on the day of Pentecost. This was a tremendous blessing, but also an incredible challenge. How could a fledgling church survive the infusion of three thousand baby Christians with an overwhelming amount of spiritual and physical needs? The key was that Jesus had left behind a leadership base, a leadership base that was capable of shepherding the needs of this new flock and quickly disciple the young Christians to maturity while still continuing to win more souls to Christ.

Not much is known about the day-to-day function of the early church, but it is not a stretch to assume that the apostles succeeded by effectively putting into practice what they had learned from Jesus. Their method of building the church was also discipling. They focused on a few, investing in them, walking with them, constantly raising up leaders who would both mentor new converts to maturity and preach to the whole world. This is why the church continued to experience rapid multiplication of disciples (Acts 4:4 and Acts 5:12-16), why the church did not stop advancing even after it was scattered (Acts 8:1-8:), and why, without universities or seminaries, the early church was able to pass on sound theology, equip and appoint evangelists, elders, and teachers and plant churches throughout the known world.   The apostles followed Jesus' way, the message and the method and it worked. It is the only way that has ever worked, for the early church accomplished what has not been accomplished since. The apostles spread the gospel throughout the known world, teaching it to every creature under heaven, within their lifetimes (Acts 17:6-7 and Colossians 1:22-23). Unless we restore discipling in our churches, we have no hope of imitating their example or accomplishing the church's ultimate goal, bringing the unadulterated gospel to the world in our lifetimes; declaring His glory among the nations, His marvelous deeds among all people (Psalm 96:3).

The Power to Win the World

Matthew 28:18-20 *"Then Jesus came to them and said, 'All authority in heaven and on earth has been given to me. Therefore go and make disciples of all nations, baptizing them in the name of the Father and of the Son and of the Holy Spirit, and teaching them to obey everything I have commanded you. And surely I am with you always, to the very end of the age.'"*

Acts 1:8 *"But you will receive power when the Holy Spirit comes on you; and you will be my witnesses in Jerusalem, and in all Judea and Samaria, and to the ends of the earth."*

Colossians 1:23 *"...This is the gospel that you heard and that has been proclaimed to every creature under heaven, and of which I, Paul, have become a servant."*

It is amazing to me that for many church leaders evangelizing the world in their lifetimes is no longer a goal, and certainly not their consuming passion. More disturbing still is among some there is a debate as to whether Jesus really expects us to accomplish this task. "Jesus did not specify a time frame," they say. "Maybe He expects it to happen over several generations and not just one."

How can such a simple command become so confusing? All we need to do is examine the example of the apostles and the first century church and all debate on this matter will cease. Jesus commanded these men to spread the gospel throughout the world and they proceeded to obey with radical urgency, sacrificing everything, risking their lives and the lives of their families, and in many cases even dying martyrs' deaths for the sake of the mission. They lived like people expecting Jesus to return any day. They lived like men who understood that unless people heard the message of the gospel there was no hope. Read the book of Acts. Look at their examples. They did not stop when their companions were murdered; they did not stop when they were scattered; they did not stop when they were imprisoned, even spreading the gospel from behind prison bars.   They were beaten, jailed, stoned, shipwrecked, disemboweled, even crucified upside down; yet, they would not cease preaching until every creature under heaven had heard the message.   Jesus told them to go to the world, the whole world and they took His words literally, they took His words personally, and they embraced His command with complete faith.   They had no money, no means, no tangible way to succeed and no historical precedent that would show that what was being asked was even possible, but they believed and their faith was rewarded.   In their lifetimes, they evangelized the known world. Jesus said to go and he said that He would be with them as they went.   For them, that was the simple recipe for success. Only faithlessness, cynicism and complacency make this any more complicated for us than it was for them. Winning the world now, in our lifetimes, is commanded, it is possible, and it is absolutely necessary.   In fact, the real issue is not reaching the lost during our lifetimes' but during theirs. Lost souls throughout the world do not have several generations for us to get the gospel to them. They will go to meet their maker long before then. They need Jesus now. God have mercy on our souls, if we are not willing to risk everything, go anywhere, and sacrifice anything to get the message to them with first century urgency.

When we speak of winning the world, we are speaking of giving every person on the planet the opportunity to hear the unadulterated gospel of Christ. Does this mean that everyone will be saved? : Of course not. The scriptures teach that the road is narrow and only a few find it (Matthew 7:13-14). Most will not choose to be saved and many will not even be open to considering the truth. Still, many will convert and everyone deserves the opportunity to hear and decide for himself. As disciples, giving them that chance is our mission and our goal.

Unlike the first century church, for us there is historical precedent for accomplishing this. I heard a preacher say this, recently, and it struck me: Our world is being evangelized every day. McDonalds is evangelizing it, as are Coca Cola and Pepsi. Since the "Dream Team" of 1992, the NBA has been successfully evangelizing the world as well, going from a very American sport to the second most popular team sport on the planet in a little over sixteen years.

The devil believes in world evangelism. The drug trade and the pornography industry have already blanketed the globe, permeating nearly every country and every cultural demographic. It is shameful how much more aggressive their peddlers are in spreading their gospel than the church is in spreading the truth. Islam believes in taking the message to the world as well, for Islam, not Christianity, is the fastest growing religion on the planet, and Muslims are far more committed to their agenda than the church has been to the Lord's. How can we turn the tide? By following in the footsteps of the first century church. Their way was Jesus' way, so if we are to duplicate their success, first we must imitate their passion and then we need to unlock the power of discipling as it relates to winning the world.

Jesus' way is to change the world one soul at a time. Mass evangelism is a great thing. Jesus preached to crowds, so obviously we need to as well, and we need to do a better job of using television, radio, and the Internet to take the message to where the lost are gathered. But although hearts can be pricked and stirred in a crowd, it is only by one soul touching another that we will ever fulfill the great commission (Matthew 28:18-20).

Matthew 28:18-20 *"Then Jesus came to them and said, 'All authority in heaven and on earth has been given to me. Therefore go and make disciples of all nations, baptizing them in the name of the Father and of the Son and of the Holy Spirit, and teaching them to obey everything I have commanded you. And surely I am with you always, to the very end of the age."*

We are told to go and make disciples of all nations. After teaching them to make Jesus Lord (become His disciples), we are to baptize them. This shows us that baptism is part of the conversion process and that there is a certain amount of knowledge, faith and conviction required for someone to be a candidate for baptism. It is not just good enough to go through some religious ritual without understanding baptism's true meaning or being mature enough to make Jesus lord.

So after conversion, what is next? In keeping with Jesus' command to the apostles, we are supposed to teach the new convert to obey everything that Jesus commanded. Teaching to obey involves more than simply passing on the concepts. It involves helping to mold the faith and the character of the young convert and showing him how to practically apply biblical principles, enabling him to take the teachings of Jesus from theory into practice. This is discipling and like Jesus and the apostles, the goal for us is to disciple young converts to maturity. We invest in them and help them master the basics. Once someone has a mastery of the basics, he can continue a lifetime of learning from the scriptures, delving into God's word, and discovering its deeper truths because he has already been weaned off of spiritual milk. Through discipling, the church not only increases membership, it multiplies workers, for once mentored to maturity, every disciple is equipped to convert the lost and disciple young converts. By investing in converts and walking with them, the church not only grows, it multiplies.

The other major aspect of discipling is training leaders. Jesus identified who among His followers could be leaders and He made them the focus of His time, teaching them His wisdom and molding their faith and character until they were mature leaders and were ready to not only convert and mentor individuals but to identify and train new leaders as well. To have a church that multiplies we must have churches that multiply leaders, for discipling is only beneficial if there are men and women who are equipped with the zeal, wisdom, and character that will make their faith worthy of imitation. If there is to be truly dynamic growth, it must be driven by an ever-increasing, dynamic leadership base. It is the death of a congregation to out baptize its leadership. It may still grow numerically for years, but its growth is fools gold. Unable to truly disciple and shepherd, the spiritual fabric of the church unravels even while the membership increases. The true measuring stick for God's church is not how many members are added each year, but how many leaders are raised up. Raising up leaders is the primary role of the evangelist and church leadership group. As evangelists, if training leaders is not our primary investment of time, we have ceased to imitate the ministry of Jesus and instead are building in a fashion that is destined to fail.

In Christianity today, the primary model for churches is the preacher model. Congregations hire full-time preachers to do the work of the church. The preacher visits the sick. The preacher mentors the flock. The preacher is responsible for growing the church. If the preacher is fortunate, he has a handful of committed members who assist him. While this is the way that most congregations function, this runs contrary to the fundamental principles of Christ's teachings and the way he built His church. We will discuss the fallacy of the preacher model in more detail later in this chapter, but at this time I'd like to contrast the preacher model and the discipling model as it relates to evangelism by using a common illustration utilized by the discipling movement *[Taken from __Discipling__ pages 29-30 __also Discipling the Multiplying Ministry__ pages 41-43]*

If a congregation hired the most zealous, most effective, preacher of all time, he would never match the effectiveness of one totally committed disciple dedicated to building Jesus' way. If the preacher were super effective and baptized a person a day for thirty-two years and the disciple baptized and discipled to maturity one person the first year and after the first year, the two disciples each converted and invested in one person and every subsequent year each disciple did the same for 32 years. This is what would happen

First Four Years:

Preacher	Disciple
1. 365	2
2. 730	4
3. 1095	8
4. 1460	16

Next Four:

5. 1825	32
6. 2190	64
7. 2555	128
8. 2920	256

By Year Thirteen:

13. 4,745	8,192

By Year Thirty-two:

32. 11,680   4.3 Billion

This simple illustration demonstrates the evangelistic power of discipling. A preacher running around converting large numbers of people creates more growth in the short term, but like the tortoise and the hare, Jesus' way works best over time. Discipling not only adds members it multiplies workers and leaders. Every disciple is a worker for the Lord and through discipling is equipped to be one. The great commission, when obeyed, has the power to reach the world.

The discipling movement has taught this principle for years but sadly, although I have been a part of discipling ministries for over two decades, I have never been part of or even heard of a ministry that really stuck with Jesus' model for the long haul without taking shortcuts. I have been around many churches with good intentions, but Jesus' way is slow. Its focus is on investing in and mentoring every single convert and identifying and investing in leaders. Helping to mature young Christians takes time and training leaders is even more time consuming. In the illustration and in reality, a ministry dedicated to Jesus' approach is just not going to see the amazing numbers in the first few years that a ministry committed to quick growth will because for the true discipling ministry, time that could be spent bringing in more and more people is spent instead on maturing the ones the congregation has, so that they can grow spiritually and assist in doing work.   Oh, the dynamic growth will come, but later and it is not the product of seeking growth but the by-product of careful, patient building. Jesus' plan is perfect, but our sinful nature often gets in the way.

Most church leaders are divided between those who are driven to grow the church and win the world and those whose focus is on maintenance. Surely Jesus wants his leaders to be among the first group, men and women whose passion is the lost, but growth without maintenance is futile. We need balance; yet, it is difficult to have that passion and also have patience. We want to save souls. We want to see hundreds and hundreds of converts come into the kingdom, so we end up chasing growth rather than having the faith that if we simply build well, growth will come.

For years I was a musician. I played the flute and over time became a jazz flutist. I remember when I first started playing jazz. I wanted to play every scale, every run, fast, but my teacher would tell me to slow it down. He'd say "Play it slow, make your tone full, play it correctly." "But what about speed?" I'd ask. "When am I going to be able to play it fast like the record?" He'd tell me not to worry about speed, never even think about it. He'd say. "If you focus on playing it right, speed will come. If you focus on speed, you'll never get it right."

This is true for music, and it is even more true for the kingdom. We do not need to worry about growth. We need to be consumed with every member being a true disciple (true disciples are evangelistic), with every young disciple being disicpled to maturity, and with leaders being raised up who can convert and mentor the crowds. If we out grow our leadership, we die. If our numbers grow faster than our spiritual maturity, we will cease to be God's kingdom and instead become a shallow imposter.

The discipling ministries I'm familiar with have traveled the following course. They would start with about forty zealous members and baptize fifty souls the first year. The second year, the now, church of ninety would baptize sixty. Sounds good, but when you look at it, the church is only marginally more effective at ninety members than it was at fifty. Why? Because very little time was spent with the fifty new converts from the first year. The work is still primarily being done by the original forty members and now, in addition to trying to convert more people they are discipling and shepherding one hundred ten young Christians. In year three, the now church of one hundred fifty baptizes forty. So, now the membership after three years is One hundred ninety. It seems impressive on the surface, but the growth is going backwards, and after closer examination, there have been only a few new leaders added or worse there have been a bunch of young Christians given leadership titles without the training. Over all, the church does not have many more real leaders or workers than it did when it started. The same committed core is trying to baptize, disciple, and mentor. Truth be told, the above illustration is incredibly generous. It does not include the large number of young disciples who leave the church and return to the world, in part because their spiritual needs have been neglected. Something has to give. How can a church continue to grow this way and how can it truly mature spiritually when little real time has been invested in the young Christians and in training new leadership? Maybe a gifted inspirational leader can squeeze growth out of this group for five, six, maybe even seven years but then what happens? At the end of the day, what kind of church has been built? Probably a church full of burned out, frustrated leaders and spiritually immature disciples. If we are honest, the above scenario describes too many churches that have sought to have a commitment to building discipling ministries. Some have seen the flaws in these ministries as a reason to abandon the principles of discipling or to lessen their commitment to world evangelism. No, the flaws exist because many of us have been more infatuated with quick growth than with carefully following Jesus' blueprint. We need to deepen our commitment to winning the world not lesson it, but be resolved to do it by paying even closer attention to the master's plan.

Having said all this, discipling works. It has the power to win the world. I lived and led a ministry in the south Bronx during the late eighties and I watched in horror the spread of the crack epidemic in the city of New York. Crack was discipling at its most powerful. In the late seventies, a new way of processing a cheaper form of cocaine was discovered and in less than a decade, the crack epidemic changed the landscape of our country. In New York, everyone was affected, regardless of race, culture or status. Virtually everyone was either on it, knew someone on it, had been robbed by someone strung out, or had to make a lifestyle change to prevent from being robbed. It was no longer safe to have a car radio; so, removable car radios became the norm. The one thing that every New Yorker knew for sure was if a person left his radio in his car, a crack addict would smash his window and steal the radio for quick cash.

In addition, a whole generation of inner city youth was tainted as far too many were lured by the opportunity to make quick money selling crack. The rise of the crack trade created an increase in gang activity and fueled the rise of gangs that would terrorize communities as diverse as South Central Los Angelos and Little Rock Arkansas. All this was well on its way in less than a decade, ugly images being recreated from city to city and from town to town.

How did it spread? Were there commercials selling crack? Were there institutions of higher learning teaching crackology? Was there a push for recruits in the print media? No. Crack was spread by one man or woman influencing another man or woman, spreading from dealer to recruit, from recruit to addict and from addict to addict. Satan believes in the power of discipling, using it everyday to win the world and spread his message. What about us? Do we believe?

God's church needs to be addicted to Jesus and we need to spread our addiction from addict to addict, from house to house, from nation to nation, until the whole world is full of the unadulterated word of God. Discipling has the power to win the world. The only questions remaining are: Do we believe and how much do we care?

The Power to Equip the Church

In addition to winning the world, discipling has the power to equip the church. The body of Christ must be equipped to finish Christ's work (John 14:12), to grow to maturity, and to love one another. The training that God's people desperately require can only be supplied through mentorship individually and in small groups.

Ephesians 4:11-13 *"It was he who gave some to be apostles, some to be prophets, some to be evangelists, and some to be pastors and teachers, to prepare God's people for works of service, so that the body of Christ may be built up until we all reach unity in the faith and in the knowledge of the Son of God and become mature, attaining to the whole measure of the fullness of Christ."* *Verse 16* *"From him the whole body, joined and held together by every supporting ligament, grows and builds itself up in love, as each part does its work."*

II Timothy 2:2 *"And the things you have heard me say in the presence of many witnesses entrust to reliable men who will also be qualified to teach others."*

According to Ephesians 4:11-13, the primary role of the church leadership (Evangelists, Pastors/Elders, Teachers, etc.) is to equip the saints for works of service. In other words, the leadership's job is to train each member how to do his job. It is not the role of the paid church leadership to go out and try to meet all the needs of the church. No individual or leadership group could accomplish this and attempting to do so will only frustrate the leaders and the church membership. The only way for the needs of Christ's body to be met and for the work of evangelizing the lost to be done is for every member to do his part. Whose job is it to visit the congregation's sick members? It is every member's job. Whose job is it to help those who are lost or feed the poor? Those tasks belong to every disciple? Yes, because the leaders are disciples first and foremost, they should be leading the way in loving the lost and the saved, but the measure of a leader is not how much of the work of the church he personally does. It is how much of the church he is able to inspire and equip to do its share. It is only when every member does his part that the church is growing and healthy. An evangelist who works for the kingdom from sun up to sun down while most of the church watches is a failure and honestly, simply doing the work himself is taking the lazy way out. Why? Because training is harder than doing. As any parent knows, more often than not, it is simpler to do the chore oneself than to teach children how to do the chore, motivate them to complete the task, and hold them accountable for doing it well. Yes, serving ones offspring is hard but parenting them is by far the harder task and is the true role of a parent. A father or mother who simply serves his children will raise spoiled, undisciplined, lazy, ingrates while the guardian who devotes his time to parenting will successfully lead his children to maturity. What is true for parents is true for church leaders as well. Discipling is their primary job.

By saying this, I'm not saying that leaders should prop up their feet and watch while the members do all the work. Such hands-off leadership is not discipling; it is neglect. We need to imitate the Master's example. Jesus served, but he used every act of service as an opportunity to teach his disciples to do the same. He called them not just to mimic His actions, but also His heart and His work ethic. He spent time with disciples instructing them concerning what lessons they should learn from His acts of service, using each act of kindness, each miracle as a teaching tool. He did not call his followers to venerate him; but rather, to imitate Him. Every act of kindness had a dual purpose. Even while He was meeting a need, he was instructing his followers how to do so, and providing an inspirational example that would motivate them to follow in His steps. Every step He took, every action, Jesus was always discipling, equipping and empowering more and more disciples to give of themselves. The mark of Jesus' greatness as a leader was not the number of people he served but the number of servants He raised up. This is the role of church leadership and discipling is our God given tool to achieve this.

Among the many lessons needing to be mastered to reach maturity, the church must learn how to practically apply scriptural principles, it must be given a sound foundation of basic theology, and it must be supplied with the tools for sharing the gospel with a lost world.   How are leaders to equip the church?   Certainly, preaching and teaching in large group settings play a part in this; yet, public ministry unaccompanied by discipling will always fall short.   In II Timothy 2:2 Timothy, the evangelist, was instructed to entrust what he had been taught to reliable men who in turn would also be able to teach others. Jesus' plan for equipping the church involves mentoring leaders individually and in small groups and those leaders in turn mentoring others in the same fashion.   This is discipling. Classes are great but without personal training, there are many lessons that Christians will never learn.   Ultimately, discipleship is caught as much as it is taught.   Faith is a spiritual virus passed on through contact, one heart touching another heart, one soul leading another to the foot of the cross.   This is how, discipling holds the key to equipping Christ's church.

The Power of Influence

Let me preface this next section by sharing what I hope by now has become obvious.   Whether we are talking about older disciples or young ones, one another relationships or discipling relationships, every disciple should desire to be influenced by other spiritual men and women. Having a guarded heart, that does not make room for the counsel of godly men and women is the product of sin, and such pride will put the individual in spiritual danger and left unchallenged act as cancer that spreads throughout the fellowship. We need each other and when we allow independence, pride, hurt and distrust to keep one another at arms length, we allow Satan a secure foothold in our hearts and weaken the body of Christ.

That being said, what is the power of discipling? The power is influence and the person holding the power is the student not the teacher. Discipling is not an issue of authority, because unless the teacher is Jesus, the mentor possesses no authority over the student and even in Jesus' case, His disciples freely chose to be molded by Him. The idea that discipling can be coerced or bullied is sheer lunacy. Discipling is a decision one man makes to allow another man to influence him. The student must not only be willing to learn, he must see his need, believe that his mentor has knowledge and faith worthy of imitation and decide to what degree he is willing to be influenced.

The role of the teacher is to have something to offer and to love sincerely from the heart. If a mature disciple sees a brother or sister in need of guidance and makes an investment of love, love is a powerful statement. It has the power to win over the skeptic, to woo the wary, and to humble the proud. The following statement is a cliché but it is true: People don't care how much you know until they know how much you care. One can have all the spirituality and wisdom in the world, but if he is not winsome, no one will be drawn to learn from him. If we learn to open wide our hearts, people will be knocking on our doors, seeking to learn what we know.

Too often, mature disciples will see a young or weak Christian struggling and be annoyed that he is not seeking the help he needs. Sometimes, the mature will seek to mentor the person even after it is clear the individual does not see the need. Please understand, when it is a matter of sin, we must get involved with one another whether or not we are invited. In Christ's church, when it is a violation of a clear command, we teach, rebuke and encourage with full authority whether someone likes it or not. But much of the mentoring disciples need from each other involves advice and the practical implementation of scriptural commands and principles. Yes, the Bible commands that I treat sisters with absolute purity, but as a single brother, how do I apply that practically to my life? Yes, I'm told to be sacrificial in my giving to God, but what are some keys to applying this? Because he is born again, a young Christian is learning everything all over again. Dating, parenting, budgeting, time management, and everything else, should all be different after we have crossed from darkness into light. The best way to learn to navigate these waters is to solicit the influence of spiritually mature brothers and sisters. Having said this, it is still true that a mature disciple who attempts to impose his influence on a disciple who does not see the need is making a huge mistake. He is doomed to frustrate himself and antagonize the one he is seeking to assist.

I Corinthians 8:1-3 *"Now about food sacrificed to idols: We know that we all possess knowledge._Knowledge puffs up, but love builds up. The man who thinks he knows something does not yet know as he ought to know. But the man who loves God is known by God."*

Proverbs 9:7 *"Whoever corrects a mocker invites insult; whoever rebukes a wicked man incurs abuse."*

Proverbs 12:1 *"Whoever loves discipline loves knowledge, but he who hates correction is stupid."*

The previous passages underscore a few principles. First, on matters of advice and experience, it is folly to seek to teach someone not eager to learn. No matter how sure we are that an individual needs help and can be spared much grief through imparting our hard earned wisdom, in the end, one can only mentor a willing student. Remember, concerning matters of sin we do not have the right to walk away. We must get involved regardless of whether the help is solicited (Matthew 18:15-17) and must pursue the matter to completion regardless of how an individual responds, but on matters of advice and influence someone has to desire to be taught. I have tried it the other way and tried to force my help on people and I have the scars to prove it. Now, I have a simple rule. I only give advice to those who want it and only seek to influence someone to the degree they desire it. Not only is this more in line with the scriptures, it eliminates unnatural pressure from my relationships in God's church.

Secondly, love is more powerful than knowledge. If we see someone who obviously needs discipling, but does not see the need, love him, serve him. Let your love melt the ice and win him over, and be amazed as this reluctant learner opens wide his heart.

Finally, the most important lesson is to leave room for God. In the end, God is everyone's primary discipler. Someone unwilling to be discipled by man will be disicpled by God. All through proverbs, the Bible labels those unwilling to listen to the wise as fools, but you know what, we all have the God given right to be foolish from time to time. Yes. It is sheer folly, pride, and stupidity (Gods words not mine Proverbs 12:1, 11:2, 13:10) for someone to reject the guidance of disciples who are wiser and more mature. Yes, learning on our own is a treacherous and painful road, but in the end, we are all living in God's classroom. If we are unwilling to learn from the tutors God places in our path, God will use our folly and our pride to teach us lessons directly, and I can tell you both from my study of the scriptures and from my own experience that these lessons while effective come at a steep price. If someone's pride makes him too hard headed to learn obvious lessons from his brothers and sisters, do not become frustrated. Love the brother or sister all the more. God is about to work on him to tenderize his prideful heart, and believe me, when that time comes, he will see his need. If you have been there loving him all along, God will lead him back to you

Conclusion

Discipling is God's plan.   It is His plan for saving the lost, equipping and maturing the church, and raising up leaders. Despite past failures, we do not have the luxury of forsaking discipling and attempting to accomplish these tasks some other way. Ultimately, the goal for every relationship is for it to mature into a true one another relationship, but achieving the goal of maturity will not happen by accident. It will happen by investing in a few, one soul touching another. This is the truth about discipling.

Passing It On

I've been a disciple over twenty-four years and in that period of time I've made more than my share of mistakes regarding relationships with brothers and sisters, particularly in the area of disicpling, and I've had some pretty horrific mistakes made on me. Still, upon reflection, I have been blessed far more by discipling than I've been hurt. I thank God for men like, Craig Cornish, John Brush, Steve Newell, Jim Brown and Don Burroughs and the time they invested seeking to aid me in improving my Christian walk and I'm especially grateful for Sam Powell and all the years and love he dedicated teaching me to how to be an evangelist and more importantly molding my faith and character as a young man.

I was raised by a single mom, who is an amazing woman. She did an incredible, selfless job being a parent to my two older brothers, my younger sister, and me. I owe so much to her. My mom's patience, her steadiness, her work ethic, her love for knowledge, her critical thinking, her willingness to serve people, her frankness, and her reverence for God laid the foundation of everything that is good in my character and was the impetus of my own quest for God. After I became a disciple, I was able to return the favor and ten years ago she became my sister in Christ. Still, for all of the wonderful things my mom did as a parent, there were holes in my development. In the end, there is only so much a mom, any mom, can teach her son about being a man.

I met Sam in May of 1986, right after graduating from college. I was all of twenty-one years old and I had moved down to Tallahassee, Florida to work for the Tallahassee Church of Christ as a campus intern for Florida A&M (FAMU) and Florida State. Sam Powell was the lead evangelist of the Tallahassee church, and in Tallahassee and later in New York, I worked with him most of the next five years, learning from him and developing a deep, life changing friendship. During that time, Sam taught me the bulk and the best of what I've learned about how to be a man of God and a minister of the gospel. I walked with him and learned how to deepen my Bible study, how to humbly confess sin, how to get out of the Spirit's way and teach the Bible in a way that was practical and relatable, how to convert non-Christians, and how to counsel disciples. Sam taught me how to preach and instructed me that while public ministry had its place it was far less important than practicing what I preached, especially in the secret places. Our classroom, was his car, the mall, campus, his living room, the grocery store, anywhere and everywhere, learning from his words, but grasping far more by the way he lived his life. I caught his faith, caught his passion for God's kingdom, his devotion to his family, his reverent submission to God because I was able to see it lived out up close and personal. I owe much of what I've learned about being an evangelist from Sam, but those were far from the most important lessons he passed on.

Shortly after meeting Sam, he invited me to have dinner at his townhouse with him and his family. It lead to me spending the night there and eventually to a weekly tradition of coming home with Sam after midweek service, eating his food, spending time with his family and then spending the night. The Powells adopted me, grafting me into their family and through their love and support, discipled my heart and character in amazing ways. I was a twenty-one year old ball of insecurity, who compensated for his fear through achievement and sought to mask it through a façade of cockiness, arrogance, and superficiality. I was a product of an ugly divorce, who had more than a few unresolved issues with his dad which resulted in a less than subtle distrust toward male authority. Like many casualties of a broken home, I had doubts about whether I could ever be a good father or be in a successful marriage. Watching Sam at home, watching him love his family, spoke directly to my fears, giving me faith in my future and a practical example of excellence. Sam was my big brother in the faith and in life, teaching me how to drive a stick, how to burp a baby, how to balance a checkbook, and so much more. He believed in me and taught me to relax and trust God, and that being myself was more than enough. I thank God for Sam not only because he discipled me in the ministry, but because he helped me develop into a man by doing nothing more special than being my friend. When I think of discipling at its best, I think of my time with Sam during those five years.

Understanding the Goal

Will Archer, a good friend and one of my favorite evangelists, has a great saying, "Always begin with the end in mind" (I'm sure he stole it from somewhere). This sentiment is the key to discipling being effective and healthy, for to restore biblical discipling, we must properly understand the goal. Having a mentor as a young man and a young minister was invaluable and If that was where it had stopped, it would have been perfect, but no one needs to be a student forever and if that phase of the relationship is unnaturally prolonged it will strain even the best friendship. Eventually, a person must be allowed to graduate and the relationship must adjust to become a friendship of equals. Hey, being Robin in the Batman and Robin team is exciting when you are a novice, but at some point Robin out grows his tights and the partnership needs to become a Batman/Superman team up, a relationship between equals with different strengths. Even the comics reflect this reality. As any comic geek knows, as he grew older, Robin got so tired of his side kick status he got rid of his old costume, changed his name to Nightwing, and moved to a different city. To your mom, whether you are two, forty-two, or sixty-two, you are always going to be her little boy or girl. Having carried you for nine months, she has earned the right to do so, but she is the only one. Everyone else needs to respect you as an adult as you mature and if they do not, it will cause conflict and unhealthy relationships. As it is in life, so it is spiritually, someone needs a mentor only for a season, but we need brothers and sisters for life. Too often, disicpling is practiced poorly simply because we do not understand our objective.

So, what is the goal of discipling? Maturity. The signs of maturity differ depending on what someone is being discipled to do. Obviously, if one is discipling a young Christian it is different than training someone in the ministry, but there are a few constants. Someone who is discipled to maturity has a mastery of the basics, the ability to build and maintain spiritual friendships, utilizing one another relationships to aid in continued growth, and the ability to be an imitator of Jesus without being dependent on human role models. The goal is to lay a foundation and wean the student off of the need for a mentor, giving him the tools to be discipled directly from Christ through the scriptures. The goal of the discipler is to aid his pupil in acquiring the faith and insight he needs to effectively walk in Christ's steps and then once the student has those skills to get out of his way and let the focus be on Christ not man. He still needs his former teacher in his life for life, but not as a mentor walking ahead of him, but as a friend walking by his side. What is the goal of discipling? Ultimately, the goal is to disciple oneself out of a job.

I Corinthians 11:1 *"Follow my example, as I follow the example of Christ."*

Philippians 4:9 *"Whatever you have learned or received or heard from me, or seen in me—put it into practice. And the God of peace will be with you."*

Ephesians 5:1-2 *"Be imitators of God, therefore, as dearly loved children and live a life of love, just as Christ loved us and gave himself up for us as a fragrant offering and sacrifice to God."*

In I Corinthians 11:1, Paul encouraged the Corinthian church to imitate the Jesus in him, the qualities in him that were worthy of being admired because those traits were Christ like. Much of the role of a mentor is to function as a role model, and for a pupil having one is both inspirational and serves as a practical example of biblical principles. As a young Christian, imitating the strengths of older disciples helped me to see the scriptures more clearly and gave me the faith that I too could grow in those areas. Overall, this is a good thing, for there is much all of us can learn from each other. When young in the faith most of us are fairly dependent on the examples we see around us in the fellowship, using them as an upward call, or in the case of negative influences, allowing them to become an excuse for settling for mediocrity in our spiritual lives. Having a mentor to disciple us and be a positive influence serves as a great asset in our quest to walk in Jesus' steps and can serve to point us in the right direction. Yet, the goal of discipling is to use this influence to point the student toward Christ not us. At the end of the day, even the best of us is deeply flawed. Anyone who puts his faith in man will be sorely disappointed. The goal of the discipler is to use his influence to instruct his charge how to more adequately be a follower of Jesus. Human examples may point us in the right direction but the goal is to become imitators of God (Ephesians 5:1) not man. As the student learns how to deepen his Bible study and increase his faith, he becomes less dependent on human example to flesh out the scriptures and learns to flesh them out for himself. The mentor becomes less and Jesus becomes more. We need brothers and sisters for life, but Jesus is the only discipler that we will never outgrow, the only one whose example is flawless, completely deserving imitation and absolute loyalty. When mature, a disciple sees Jesus clearly and stays focused on the Lord regardless of what others are doing around him. If all his friends lose faith, the mature disciple holds steady, and if all his spiritual heroes fall from grace, the mature disciple fixes his gaze on the one super hero who will always inspire: Jesus.

On to Maturity

As stated in chapter two, discipling is designed to meet five specific needs:

I.   It is the Bible's way of training preachers and prophets

II.   It is the way of equipping and raising up leaders

III.   It is the way to convert non-Christians

IV.   It is the way of shepherding, equipping, and maturing baby Christians

V.   It is a way of imparting specific knowledge or skills. (Such as newlyweds being mentored by a veteran couple)

While the specifics involved in discipling vary depending on the need being met, spiritual seasoning is always the goal. The objective is to lay a foundation through spiritual mentorship that will allow the young Christian, the new preacher, etc. to go on to maturity.

Maturity is not perfection and it is not reaching some superhuman standard of consistency. What we are looking for from the individuals we are helping needs to be attainable and in keeping with the scriptures. Those who are teachers need to give some thought to what they are trying to achieve. What does it mean to disciple a young Christian to maturity? How long should it generally take? What does it mean to train someone to shepherd a small group, and what are the signs that he is ready? What are the signs that someone has been adequately discipled to be an evangelist? If we do not have a clear picture of where we are going it is impossible to get there.

In the ministry that I currently lead, we have a very specific vision of what it means to disciple a young Christian to maturity and it is our belief that in most cases an adult convert can attain this after being disicipled a year or less although with teens and young college students, the investment is generally much longer. As an example, below, I share what our congregation generally looks for and what we are attempting to attain when we speak of mentoring a young convert to maturity. The objective here is not to advocate our methodology but to share our thought process.

> **Hebrews 5:11-Hebrews 6:3** *"We have much to say about this, but it is hard to explain because you are slow to learn. In fact, though by this time you ought to be teachers, you need someone to teach you the elementary truths of God's word all over again. You need milk, not solid food! Anyone who lives on milk, being still an infant, is not acquainted with the teaching about righteousness. But solid food is for the mature, who by constant use have trained themselves to distinguish good from evil.*
>
> *Therefore let us leave the elementary teachings about Christ and go on to maturity, not laying again the foundation of repentance from acts that lead to death,_and of faith in God, instruction about baptisms, the laying on of hands, the resurrection of the dead, and eternal judgment. And God permitting, we will do so."*

There are five objectives that we seek to achieve in discipling a young Christian to maturity and they also serve as a way of measuring whether a disciple is reasonably mature:

5 Keys...

I. Must Possess a Sound Doctrinal Understanding of the Basics:

(Hebrews 6:1-2). According to the writer of Hebrews there is basic theological understanding that a disciple must possess in order to be considered mature. Every disciple of Christ should have a good working knowledge of these areas so that he can progress to maturity by moving from spiritual milk to solid food. While I do not believe that Hebrews 6 is an exhaustive list, it does give us a starting point and an idea of what types of topics should be considered basics. Some of what we look for...

A. Baptisms/ False doctrine: In the first century and today, there are other baptisms being taught in the religious world other than Jesus's baptism. What does the Bible truly teach about baptism and what is the distinction between the one true baptism of Ephesians 4:1-5 and other baptisms that exist in the religious world. Understanding the difference between sound doctrine about conversion and false doctrine is an essential part of the basics.

B. Who is lost and who is saved: Being saved is about what's right not who's right, but what about "Christian" groups that teach a different way to be saved than the scriptures?   Are they saved? How important is doctrine?   How can we be prepared for the judgment to come if we cannot effectively answer these questions (Hebrews 6:3)

C. The Holy Spirit: What does the Bible teach about the Holy Spirit, about the gifts of the spirit, about the laying on of hands?   How do I know I have the Holy Spirit?   In (Heb 6:1-2), this is considered basic knowledge, milk not solid food.

D. Repentance (Hebrews 6:2): What does it mean to repent?   What are the acts that were leading the convert to death?   How can he be victorious against them? Etc.

E. Other areas that we cover: Christian Dating, Christian Marriage, What is the Kingdom, Discipling

& the One Another Way, Grace, What It Means to be a Member, and Sacrificial Giving

II. Must Be Totally Committed:

Simply put, Jesus must be Lord (Luke 9:23-26). In poker terms it means being all in, not perfect but 100% committed. Sometimes, we are weak, sometimes we struggle, but we must be fully committed. What are some signs of that commitment?

A. Commitment to the Body: Someone who is mature in the Lord has deep convictions about being present every time the body meets.

B. Must be able to weather spiritual storms: Part of developing mature conviction about commitment is acquiring the ability to weather storms spiritually without lessening one's discipleship

C. Learning to identify and use spiritual gifts: Part of helping a young Christian to mature in his commitment is helping him to identify and use his spiritual gifts to build up the body of Christ. A sign of maturity is identifying one's niche and being emotionally vested.

III. Must Be Able to Distinguish Good from Evil (Hebrews 5:14):

He must have the discernment to recognize sin, the conviction to deny it and to confess and repent when he falls.

IV. Must Be Able to Initiate and Build Spiritual Friendships

He must have conviction about building and maintaining strong Proverbs 27:17, Proverbs 18:24 friendships and practicing the one another commands.

V. Must Be Able to Study the Bible with People

The expectation is that any disciple should be able to teach someone how to become a disciple. Everyone is not going to be a Bible scholar or be the most gifted Bible teacher; yet, one does not need to be in order to show someone from the scriptures how to have a relationship with God. In Matthew 9:36-38, Jesus looked at the harvest of souls before Him and lamented that the workers are few. As we disciple, we multiply workers because by the time someone has been discipled to maturity, he should be a productive worker for the Lord.

To help our young Christians with their growth, when each is converted, a mature disciple volunteers to disciple him. As a congregation, We are devoted to this, believing that, as a family, we are worse than negligent if individual attention is not given to each born again soul. The volunteer commits to studying the Bible with the new member once a week, investing time and helping with the fundamentals. This mentor is not the young converts only relationship, but he is the one who has accepted the responsibility for personal training and instruction. In my experience, if we invest in people, a foundation can be laid in months not years, but if we do not invest, disciples can be around for decades and never mature. When the time is right, the mentorship concludes, but the friendship continues for a lifetime. This is our approach, but again, the reason I'm sharing this is not to persuade others to adopt our specific plan for discipling young Christians. The point is that we come up with a plan. No matter how we go about accomplishing it, we need to have the conviction that discipling; biblical discipling, must be restored in Christ's church. Sermons and classes are useful, but by themselves, they can never replace the personal

touch. Passing it on, one soul touching another, is how we are
going to grow the church and win the world.

A Company of Prophets

How are leaders to be trained? Elijah and Elisha, Barnabas and
Paul and Paul and Timothy are all examples of the power of
discipling when it comes to raising up leaders. By walking with
an older more mature prophet, new prophets are forged.
Evangelists, teachers, and elders need to be discipled over a
period of time before they are given titles and responsibility.
These are the most important jobs in the world and need to be
treated as such. Any shortcuts in this area will always have
devastating repercussions on the body of Christ. Formal
theological training is great, but it will not mold character, it will
not measure faith, and it will not test for integrity. We will never
improve on God's plan. It was the Spirit who wrote, "He who
walks with the wise grows wise" (Proverbs 13:20), so there is no
substitute for the intimacy of Jesus' training method. We must
pour out our lives, investing in the next generation if we hope to
see new prophets moving the gospel forward.

Like Jesus, we need to focus on a few, two or three young
leaders with whom we will open wide our hearts. As an
evangelist, this is my primary role, my most important task, to

raise up young men and women who can inspire and shepherd God's people and preach the gospel to a lost world (If you're wondering I'm talking about women preaching to women and assisting the male leadership in shepherding the church
I Timothy 2:11-13). If my life is too full or too busy for this work, then I do God's church a disservice. Faithful, inspirational leaders are an endangered species, and there is no more important task on the planet than lighting the flame for a company of young prophets.

Christ's Way or No Way

Discipling has its place. The relationships that mature disciples need to have are one another relationships, but without discipling how are disciples to mature? As with all things, it is up to each individual to delve into the scriptures and develop his own convictions about this topic and it is up to each individual congregation's leadership to determine how to best implement disicpling within the church in their care, but what cannot be debated is that Biblical discipling must be restored.

We will never fail to obey scriptures without suffering consequences, for God's plans are perfect; His ways ensure victory. If Jesus practiced discipling as He equipped and mentored His apostles, who are we to try and develop a better way? We cannot. There is a weakness in our churches that all of our best thinking cannot fix, a lack of soundness that even the most powerful sermons cannot rectify. It is not some new scheme that we need to devise. We need to go back to the ancient ways, Jesus' way, and rediscover the truth about discipling, and once we rediscover it, let us pass it on.

Why We Cannot Fail

The church is alive. It is not a human organization or a man made structure, but the living breathing body of Christ. Christ's church is meant to be a family, not a business or an army; thus, everything about the body is relational. Our spirituality revolves around our bond with Christ and one another. Much of the success and failure of our journey is determined by the quality of our relationships.

With this in mind, the Holy Spirit wrote the one another commands, serving as both a road map and our lifeline. We ignore them at our peril, but when these scriptures are obeyed, we unlock the secrets of the one another way and the power of Christ's love in our fellowship. We cannot afford to fail in the restoration of these commands because so much depends on our diligence in this matter.

The Church Is Crying Out

Whether or not we realize it, the church is crying out for a revival and the one another way contains the key. There can be no true discipleship without discipling, nor can there be true brotherhood without deep spiritual friendships. There is a loneliness in our churches, an emptiness that haunts many of our members even while they are singing in a pew, in a crowded room. Being present does not make us connected. And without true connection, we are simply familiar strangers gathered in a room, singing out of hymnals. We all want the church to be warmer, more loving, more sensitive to needs...more of a family, and at times we are simply standing around looking for someone else to fix us. The simple truth is that the secret to fixing the church requires individuals making a personal investment in one another. We need to focus on a few, pouring out our hearts, loving without limits. The spirit is waiting on us, dying to deliver us from lukewarmness, stagnation, and mediocrity. We are the problem and the solution. Individually, we must decide to embrace the scriptures, trust our Savior, and love one another deeply, unconditionally, and intimately.

Proverbs 18:24 "*A man of many companions may come to ruin, but there is a friend who sticks closer than a brother.*"

Proverbs 27:17 *"As iron sharpens iron, so one man sharpens another."*

As mentioned elsewhere, the above passages outline the heart of the matter. The secret is that we have to both desire and labor for spiritual friendships, friendships whose goal is to sharpen each other for the Lord and we are going to have to focus on a few in order to build depth.   In any congregation, it is easy to have companions, but it takes extreme dedication to build life-changing friendships. If we will make that investment, we will create a revival in the church by sharpening each other one soul at a time.

The World Is Waiting

The church needs revival and the world needs hope, and there is nothing, no philosophy, no economic plan, no political movement, that can help the world except Jesus. While the church is trying to decide what it believes about world evangelism, Satan is evangelizing the world.   While our fellowships are splintering, the dark one is solidifying his hold. While we are debating the merits of discipling, Lucifer is utilizing discipling to spread his message and corrupt communities, one soul at a time. Satan is using worldly family members to disciple our brothers, using co-workers to woo our sisters, and using classmates to corrupt our children, one person touching another, mentoring each one down the wide road, the road to Hell. We are Christ's body, the only hope for this lost world. We are the hands that Jesus uses to mend hearts, the lips he uses to rebuke sin, and the feet that He uses to bring the gospel to the world, and the world is waiting, waiting for our response, waiting for us to act.

We will not multiply the gospel throughout the world without restoring Biblical discipling in our churches and believing in the power of God's plan. Every individual deserves to hear the true unadulterated gospel of Christ before he dies. They deserve it, Jesus wants it, and He has provided the way, a way of multiplying both workers and leaders, a way to turn this world upside down and tear the devil's kingdom down. I truly believe that we will rally around the cause of world evangelism and with humility heal our fractured fellowships or God will raise up a movement of Godly men and women from our ashes who have the faith and the passion to answer the call.

Too many leaders are trying to maintain the church rather than to advance it, are leading out of fear rather than with vision, and are making decisions based on finances rather than faith. We live in a time of too many priests and too few prophets, where the call is comfort rather than sacrifice, and where great numbers are building their paneled houses (Haggai 1:4) while the Lord's house is ruined and corrupted by the disease of complacency. Our youth are uninspired because radical faith, rather than skillfully crafted speeches and empty homilies, is what moves them. The youth will not be stirred until the prophets return. The world is waiting. We are on the winning team. It is time that we recapture the fire to take the gospel to every nation, every city, and every town and refocus on the mission that has been given to us.

One another fellowship is the answer. Through spiritual friendships, we will find our zeal one heart at a time, one soul at a time, passing along faith like a virus. Discipling is the answer. We will multiply workers and leaders, investing in each other, growing like a mustard seed, toppling the gates of Satan's kingdom. The one another way is the hope for a lost world. Through it, we will win this world for Christ. Why? : Because, in Christ, success is always guaranteed.

Now Is the Time

"It's Time."

It's time. It's past time. It's overtime
It's sudden death, do or die

It's time.

While we've been waiting
The world is still lost
While we've been selfish
The world is still lost
It's time.

We've been busy so busy too busy to share.
We've been fighting each other too burdened to care.
 We've looked at the price and blinked at the cost
And while we've been waiting,
The world is still lost.

Brothers and sisters moms and dads
Co-workers, neighbors, strangers, old friends,
The janitor, the doctor, even your boss
They all need the cross.
They all need the cross.
And while we we've been busy,
The world is still lost.

It's time. It's past time. It's overtime.
Time to wake up, time to shake up,
To stir up, to raise up, to lift up, to look up,

It's time.

Brothers and sisters, it's time.

After His resurrection, Jesus commissioned eleven men to take His message to the world, armed with only the scriptures, the Spirit, and a plan. What he gave them was more than enough and through Him they evangelized the world in their lifetimes. Now, it is our turn. The one another scriptures have the power to pump the blood of Christ through Christ's body awakening our faith, discipling is the plan that will carry the gospel forward, and the Holy Spirit is a force that nothing in all creation, in heaven or on earth can resist. We are in a fight that we were born to win, having our Father's Spirit, His spiritual DNA within us. Let us embrace the one another way, ride the wave of revival and watch our Lord usher in a miracle during our lifetimes. In Christ we will be closer than brothers. In Christ we cannot fail.

Closer Than a Brother

Below is a list of scriptures for further study. While this list is far from exhaustive, it should provide for much fruitful study. Enjoy.

Love	Unity	Grace/Forgiveness
I Peter 4:8	Psalm133:1	Proverbs 17:9
John 13:34-35	John 17:20-23	Proverbs 17:14
John 15:12	Ephesians 4:2-3	Romans 14:13
Romans 13:8	Romans 12:16	Galatians 6:2
I Corinthians 12:25	Romans 15:5	I Thessalonians 5:15
II John 1:5	Galatians 5:15	I John 1:7
I Thessalonians 3:12	Galatians 5:26	Romans 12-14-21
I Thessalonians 4:18	Romans 12:5	Matthew 5:38-39
II Thessalonians 1:3	I Corinthians 1:10	Matthew 5:43-48
I Peter 1:22 I	I Corinthians 12:25	
John 3:11	Philippians 4:2	
I John 3:16	I Peter 3:8	
I John 3:23	John 17:20-21	
I John 4:7		
I John 4:11-12		
I John 4:19-21		

Forgiveness	Confession	Compassion
Ephesians 4:32	Proverbs 28:13	I Thessalonians 4:18
Colossians 3:13	James 5:16	Ephesians 4:32
Romans 15:7	I John 1:9	Colossians 3:12
I Thessalonians 5:15	Numbers 5:5-7	

Advice	Patience/Humility	The Tongue
Proverbs 11:2	Proverbs 18:13	Ephesians 4:29
Proverbs 11:14	Ephesians 4:2	Proverbs 18:21
Proverbs 12:15	Philippians 2:1-5	Proverbs 26:20
Proverbs 13:10	Galatians 5:26	Proverbs 16:28
Proverbs 14:12	Romans 14:13	James 3:1-12
Proverbs 15:22	Ephesians 5:21	Ephesians 5:19
Proverbs 19:20	Colossians 3:13	James 4:11
I Kings 12:1-33	Ecclesiastes 7:8	James 5:9
		Proverbs 15:4
		Proverbs 10:19
		Colossians 3:8

184

Teaching/Correction	Friendship	Discipling
Proverbs 12:1	Proverbs 17:17	Proverbs 28:26
Proverbs 13:18	Proverbs 18:24	Proverbs 13:20
Proverbs 15:12	Proverbs 27:17	Matthew 28:19-20
Colossians 3:16 I	Ephesians 4:8-12	Proverbs 19:8
I Thessalonians 5:11	Ecclesiastes 4:8-12I I	I Corinthians 4:17
Hebrews 3:13	I Samuel 20: 41-42	I Kings 19:19-21
Romans 15:14	I Samuel 23:15-18	Mark 3:13-18
Romans 14:19	II Corinthians 2:12-13	John 15:13-17
	Ruth 1:16-18	

Truth	Conflict
Proverbs 28:23	Matthew 18:15-17
Proverbs 27:5-6	Matthew 5:23-24
Proverbs 4:25	I Corinthians 6:1-11
Proverbs 4:15	Proverbs 18:17
Colossians 3:9	
Proverbs 12:19	
Ephesians 4:15	
Ephesians 4:25	

Encouragement	Serving
Romans 12:10	Galatians 5:13
Hebrews 10:24	I Peter 4:9
Hebrews 10:25	John 13:1-17
Hebrews 3:13	
I Thessalonians 5:11	

Bibliography

Coleman, Robert E. The Master Plan of Evangelism 2nd ed. Grand Rapids: Fleming H. Revell a division of Baker Book House Company, 1963.

Ferguson, Gordon. Discipling. Woburn: Discipling Publications International, 1997

Jones, Milton Lee. Discipling the Multiplying Ministry. Ft. Worth: Star Bible & Tract Corp., 1982

The Hebrew-Greek Key Word Study Bible. Chattanooga: AMG Publishers, 1996

"Adam Clarke Commentary." http://www.studylight.org/com/acc/view.cgi?book=1sa&chapter=018 (March 3, 2007)

Printed in the United States
147263LV00002B/55/P